BAD FEELINGS, BAD BUSINESS

BAD FEELINGS, BAD BUSINESS

Don't Let Unseen Emotions Destroy Career Success

Richard M. Contino

York House Press

Library of Congress Control Number: 2013931286

ISBN: 978-0-9855508-9-9

Visit yorkhousepress.com

Printed in the United States of America

Dedication

To my wife and partner, Penny, and our two great kids, May-Lynne and Matthew

CONTENTS

Take Control of Your Future—Acknowledge Business Reality and
Trust Your Gut
Common Emotional Issues that Drive Bad Decisions
Summary

ABOUT THE AUTHOR

Richard M. Contino, Esq. is an attorney, business consultant and independent businessman, with degrees in aeronautical engineering and law from Rensselaer Polytechnic Institute (B. Aero. Eng.), the University of Maryland School of Law (J.D.) and the New York University Graduate School of Law (LL.M.). He is the author of nine business and financial books, as well as a motivational speaker and business seminar leader.

Following a tour of duty with the US Air Force as a JAG captain, Dick worked on Wall Street and in Corporate America before becoming an entrepreneur and independent businessman, having founded or co-founded eight businesses. Several of his companies advise domestic and international businesses, as well as financial institutions.

Dick is a painter and martial artist, living with his wife, Penny, an entrepreneur, and their son, Matthew, in Westchester, New York. His daughter, May-Lynne, a budding entrepreneur, works with Penny and lives in California.

INTRODUCTION

If you're not where you want to be in business, *Bad Feelings, Bad Business* is for you. There is no doubt that if you have the desire, you have the talent, and only one thing stands in your way—how you think about work and business and the people you meet there. Change this and success will follow, quickly and easily.

You may find this hard to believe from your vantage point now, but if you're up for the challenge of taking on some powerful and game-changing new awareness skills, this book will place you in the driver's seat.

Bad Feelings, Bad Business is based on years of work spent searching for answers as to why career or busiess success is often so elusive. Why did some endeavors work almost without effort? And why did others fail in spite of hard work and how right they seemed? Every aspect of the business process was explored in the process. Books, courses, management consultants, and executive coaches all promised concrete answers. Time and time again the results were the same—excitement that a real solution was found, followed, invariably, by disappointment and frustration.

Many personal experiences informed me. Once, during a particularly frustrating business negotiation, as I struggled to bring all parties to a meeting of the minds, it suddenly occurred to me that my negotiating partner and I were on the wrong track. While the business proposal before us made absolute sense for all concerned, getting to an agreement was proving tough. During a lunch break, as everyone relaxed, it became apparent that inner emotional needs might be the stumbling blocks. Although he didn't come right out and say it, one member of the opposing side hinted that he wished he had gone to a better school and pursued an advanced degree. Although everyone respected his business skills, he apparently felt inferior to some at the meeting he thought had a better educational pedigree. His hang-up surfaced as "my way or the highway" style demands that slowed progress. Armed with this insight, my partner and I returned to the negotiating table and took a different tack with our opponent—less confrontational and more collaborative, willing to defer to him, so he felt more in control and less inclined to imagine we were "talking down to him".

Experiences like these transformed my casual interest in unconscious behaviors to a deep exploration of the underlying emotional issues that often, without our knowing, dictate career success or failure. The journey has been eye-opening and resulted in tools you can add, with just a few hours of reading, to your career toolkit.

As you might now begin to suspect, the first step to predictable success is to come to terms with the how and why emotional issues dictate success or failure—something never taught in business schools and ignored by the business community. And the best place to start is with the widely held belief that emotions have no place in business, and, therefore, they're not a factor. This belief is not only a critical misconception, but is the reason for virtually every business failure—and success! The fact is that emotions underlie and control every aspect of the business process. So, if you have not explored the controlling aspect emotions, yours and those of the people around you, have in the business process, this book will revolutionize your thinking.

Bad Feelings, Bad Business will not only tell you why and how underlying emotional agendas control the business process, but it will show you what to do to remove all progress blocks—in a simple and straight-forward manner. You'll learn, for example, unique ways to increase your emotional awareness so you can achieve predictable and positive results immediately; something that will give you an unprecedented competitive edge in business. You'll also learn how to instantly spot the obvious emotional progress roadblocks, and how to look for ever-present clues to the existence of the not-so-obvious ones. In a nutshell, you'll gain practical information and awarenesses to dramatically improve your business approach and increase success opportunities, such as:

- Managing feelings for success
- Spotting back stabbers and other people trying to do you in
- Overcoming life preconditioning and common beliefs that block success
- Critical emotional self-awareness approaches for unblocking potential
- How and why emotional needs often override financial security
- Why some people unknowingly sabotage themselves
- How to spot roadblocking patterns in people you depend on
- Making sure you're not being held back by a destructive boss
- Identifying clues to hidden agendas that block progress
- How to turn the tables on people intentionally getting in your way
- Techniques for super decision making
- How to access your creative unconscious for business solutions

Concepts and techniques, however, are not enough for lasting progress. You have to actually experience positive results for yourself in your business environment. Toward this end, *Bad Feelings, Bad Business* makes extensive use of special hypothetical business situations and practical exercises you can use in day-to-day business to both verify and benchmark what will work best for you. The more effort you put in applying concepts and strategies, the faster you'll progress. You will be unstoppable—and that is a guarantee. See you at the top!

Dick Contino

Chapter 1

BUSINESS AND EMOTIONS

The Real Business Challenge is You

If you are not where you want to be in business, no doubt you're acting and thinking in a way that's blocking your progress. Change that, and success will follow—immediately. Hard to imagine? Well, see what you think after you finish this book. And, if you agree, you'll then have the tools to do something about it.

Keep the following idea in mind as you read: Success happens naturally when we don't get in our own way. Failure is a choice—one that you don't have to make.

The Premise — Emotions Control All Business Decisions

With the endless supply of how-to books and business courses and the availability of top consultants, do you ever wonder why so many businesses fail and careers fall short? It's simple. None addresses the real cause of failure—destructive thoughts and feelings. As a result, in effect, we accept failure as a way of life in business.

Here's the reality: All business decisions are dictated by emotional needs. And rarely do we see, or for that matter want to see, how certain of these needs can corrupt our business decisions. Keeping our head in the sand, however, is falsely comforting—and a formula for disaster.

I'm not suggesting that all emotionally-driven business decisions are bad, but only that ignoring the possibility of ever-present emotional components could cripple your ability to effectively take right actions or make right decisions. Ignoring potential emotional agendas in business is like ignoring what your competition is doing.

Why We Miss the Obvious

When you think about it, it's easy to understand why we miss seeing how and when counterproductive thoughts and feelings cripple businesses and our careers. It stands to reason that emotional issues have no place in business and, therefore, we often operate under the misconception that they aren't the controlling factor. Nothing could be further from the truth. Our emotional needs, good and bad, are in play in every step of the business process. When emotional agendas are destructive, failure is guaranteed. When they're productive, success is assured.

BREAKTHROUGH INSIGHT: It's upsetting to think we might be actively self-destructive in business. But by not considering this as a possibility when we're not moving forward, we miss obvious ways self-destructive agendas in others and in ourselves block progress.

I'm not suggesting that everyone in business is so hampered by roadblocking emotional issues that they cannot reach their full potential. Clearly, there are people who can, even in the face of common destructive thoughts and feelings—in themselves and in others—and in spite of a full understanding of how and why self-limiting needs and agendas can cripple progress. For a variety of reasons, they're the lucky ones. In some cases they may have had positive and successful role models. In other cases possibly success was an emotional necessity, driven by, say, childhood poverty.

The Hidden Business Killer — Destructive Agendas

Unfortunately, even when we understand that destructive emotional agendas can exist in all aspects of the business process as a possibility, it's extremely difficult to allow ourselves to see when they're in play. And that is understandable. Considering that they might exist can force us to question everything we've been taught by our parents, teachers and mentors about how business works and what we need to do to get ahead. So we either ignore the signs of their existence or reformat what we see into something that we can live with emotionally—often completely unconsciously.

Here's the challenge: If we face the possibility that the business process is often driven by irrational and illogical counterproductive thoughts and feelings, we have to come to terms with an unfortunate truth—that it may not always be possible to do what makes business sense. The fact is that destructive emotional needs and feelings can totally block your progress no matter what you do or say. Profits may be irrelevant. The best course of action may be irrelevant. This is not a welcome thought for anyone trying to do well.

BREAKTHROUGH INSIGHT: Some crippling business misconceptions can be so deeply embedded in our unconscious mind that uncovering and changing them may not be possible without professional guidance. The thinking that held you back is not the thinking that will move you forward.

If you're stuck and beginning to suspect that you may have been unknowingly victimized by well-meaning folks who actively imposed self-destructive beliefs on you, take comfort. You're not alone. These beliefs, assumptions not based on hard facts or illusions, are passed on from generation to generation and result in systemic emotional business blind spots, something I'll discuss further in Chapter 2. And, because they were imposed on us at a time when we didn't have the knowledge or experience to properly evaluate them, we accepted them as absolute truths. Rarely, if ever, do we question them. Rest assured, once you accept the possibility that counterproductive emotional needs could block your ability to progress, you'll quickly learn to spot times when they may be getting in the way. And, once they have been identified, you'll learn to work around the ones you can't eliminate.

The First BIG Step: Examining Your Beliefs

To move yourself forward you must examine and re-examine every belief you have in business—continually. When you do this, however, expect that a part of you, that which in effect is your destructive unconscious, will challenge your efforts at every step of the way. Its main job is to keep you emotionally comfortable, so it masterfully reformats everything you see and hear in a way that you can accept, or offers up ready rationalizations for things that would otherwise be upsetting to confront head on. So, simply, if unconsciously or, even consciously, you don't want face something, your inner monster will block it out completely or reframe it so you can comfortably process it. The net result is that then you're easily held hostage to destructive emotional agendas and kept behind the business eight ball—way behind.

Unfortunately, your inner monster is all-powerful, with virtually an iron-fist hold over your conscious existence. So, what can you possibly do? Trick your thought process so you can process information that may run counter to your non-productive beliefs, such as information that may differ from how you think business or the world is or should be.

So, how do you trick your inner monster to end-run the control it has over you? Don't try to accept any new idea or concept as an absolute truth. Make a conscious effort to only consider it as a possibility. The same holds true for any existing belief you have which you want to re-examine. Simply entertain the possibility that the belief may not be well-founded. As silly as this may sound, it works. Taking something in as a possibility can end-run your unconscious blocking mechanism and allow you eventually to see what's really in front of you.

BREAKTHROUGH INSIGHT: Accept the possibility that in any given problem situation you or someone else could unknowingly be undermining both your efforts and theirs, even if it makes no absolute sense. That sets the stage for preventing misleading or other distracting thoughts from hindering your ability to move forward—thoughts such as "I must be too stupid to understand," or "He could not possibly be thinking something so absurd."

How Can You Spot a Hidden Agenda?

No one can really be sure what drives a given business decision. This can be true even when you're the decision-maker. The key, however, is to learn to uncover any hidden destructive agendas that could impact a solid business decision or effort by identifying clues to when they may be in play, something I'll explore further in Chapter 6. Just to get you thinking now, however, a clue that the decision may be based on a counterproductive emotional agenda might be when someone does something that makes no business sense, such as when a manager hires someone clearly unqualified for a job—something that could signal that his priority could be to keep his job position safe rather than make the best business choice.

Let's Take Your Emotional Temperature

Do you watch Entertainment Tonight or other so-called celebrity gossip shows, gawking at all the glamorous folks who seem to have it all? Do you closely follow their lives, as they leap from one marriage to another—or from one problem to another— all the while having one apparent success after another? If so, the next time you're watching one of your favorite shows, take particular note of your feelings and thoughts. Chances are you're relating to a fantasy life or looking for a way to feel better about yourself by comparing yourself to others who have a harder time than you. Either could be a clue to something within you that is blocking you from living up to your potential.

BREAKTHROUGH INSIGHT: Real success comes when all personal inner conflict disappears, particularly about your unique talents or true value. This is less likely to happen when you're measuring yourself against others. But it will happen when you are on the right track for you—and you'll feel it. Then, nothing you see or hear will make you feel inadequate. You'll no longer put your value in the hands of others to trash at will.

Not you? Ok, how about this? Do you often follow in awe the careers of wealthy people to see what you should be doing to better yourself? This, of course, would certainly not be all bad, as long as you're brutally honest with yourself about why you do this. But, when we engage in so-called idol worship, it's often simply a way our inner monster discourages us from reaching our potential. And doing so prevents us from accessing and using our unique talents—something everyone is born with. So trying to imitate others can be a mistake and can slow you down. Their talents and inclinations may be quite different. To prosper, you must find your own inner path using your own innate gifts—and forget about trying to follow the so-called success leaders.

BREAKTHROUGH INSIGHT: Did a doubt about having hidden talents flash through your mind? If so, this is a clue to how you're holding yourself back. Doubts often surface when we resist a belief change. So, when they surface, dig deeper to understand what's really behind them. If they are based on irrational fears, these fears will unfairly get in the way of progress. Use your doubts as trustworthy clues to ways you limit yourself.

One more question. Do you ever find yourself adhering to beliefs that you have never questioned? Beliefs that come from other people and not from your own experience, such as it's hard to succeed in business? That to find success you must have a special education or go to a top college? Or be in the right place at the right time? If so, and you've never questioned what really are self-limiting beliefs, chances are good you won't make the necessary breakthroughs. And years of frustration could push you to quit trying, believing that achieving your dreams is just not in the cards for you. If that happens, the resulting emotional and psychological toll can be great, even to the point of leaving you feeling like a loser. This does not have to happen!

5

BREAKTHROUGH INSIGHT: Don't automatically accept society's rhetoric about the measure of success or happiness. It's usually generated by self-indulgent people who are actually frightened by life's realities and its unknowns—people who frantically try to control outcomes and the people around them to ease their fears and bad feelings.

If You Have the Desire You Have the Talent

There is absolutely no doubt that if you have a desire to achieve a particular goal in business you have the talent to achieve it. So, as I've said, if you are not where you want to be at this stage in your career or your business endeavors, one thing is clear—you are getting in your own way.

While it's hard to make a general statement about what the roadblocks to your progress could be, a major contributing factor is likely your failure to risk getting out of your emotional comfort zone. And that may show up, for example, as an inability to work with positive people who can make things happen, simply because doing so might shine a light on your bad feelings about yourself. If this is the case, push forward. You'll soon discover that all the uncomfortable feelings you may be avoiding will drop away.

Your First Awareness Breakthrough Exercise

The following exercise will help you start the process of clearing your mind of business illusions and other beliefs not based on hard facts that are a roadblock to progress. It's one of many I'll provide to enable you to make the belief breakthroughs necessary to change your "luck" in business.

Over the next week be open to the possibilities that:

People in business often act in self-destructive ways.

Business decisions are emotionally driven, even when profit, growth or career objectives are put at risk.

Make a written note of these two possibilities and review them at the start of each business day. As you go through the day, jot down any immediate thoughts or feelings you have relating to these possibilities as they occur, and then review them at the end of the day. By waiting until day's end, you'll give yourself a chance to fully and consciously process anything you discover. If you forget to do any of this on any given day, no matter the reason, use that as a strong clue that you may be actively roadblocking your progress. The point here is to start to identify your thoughts—particularly the ones that flit by with little or no awareness on your part—and your feelings.

BREAKTHROUGH INSIGHT: If you're not where you want to be very suspicious of all of your rationalizations at this point. In fact, for now, entertain the possibility that your rational thoughts, your logic, may be faulty—that they are so tainted by your destructive or self-limiting needs that they may be hampering your business progress.

How We're Going to Proceed

This book pulls together the concept of emotions in business in a number of ways. It explains how and why emotions play a controlling part in business failure and success. In order for your business thinking to evolve, however, theory is not enough. You must know how to apply the theory in a practical way. So, to enable you to do this, you'll learn unique approaches to business emotional self-analysis. In addition, you'll learn how to make awareness adjustments so you can develop strategies that will increase your business effectiveness. In effect, this material is going to put you in touch with what a part of you already knows—how to prosper. It's going to teach you how to rely on your inner genius rather than always looking to outside experts to verify whether or not you're on the right path. Where important, earlier key concepts will be summarized in slightly different ways to frame new concepts as they are discussed to ensure that any unconscious self-limiting tendencies do not cause you to miss information that will help you to progress.

At strategic points in the book, you'll have the opportunity to reinforce the awareness concepts presented using specific exercises, similar to the one in this chapter. The exercises are designed to help you apply the book concepts in your work world. By taking the time to work through each of them, you will reinforce and accelerate the development of your awareness skills. Each exercise will be followed by an analysis of controlling emotional factors which may be involved to provide you with a basis for analyzing any other emotional issues that you discover on your own. A word of caution: As you work with these awareness tasks, do not jump ahead to the analysis before you are told to do so. The tasks have been designed to lead you carefully through potentially unconscious destructive or adverse conditioning or patterning. If you know too much too soon, you may unknowingly get in your own way. Never forget: We all have a limiting unconscious inner self and it is creative and powerful. It wants to keep us where we are.

A Development Diary Suggestion

I suggest writing your thoughts and feelings down as you go through each exercise. This will enhance your ability to quickly integrate the concepts into your awareness. If this is something you decide to do, I recommend that you purchase a notebook to use as your Development Diary. Don't pick one that is just any color. Select a color that appeals to you at a gut level. This will be your personal Diary. Do not let anyone read it. Use this Diary to record your honest thoughts and feelings as you work with each awareness exercise.

BREAKTHROUGH INSIGHT: As you read this book, pay particular attention to reactions you have to those ideas you agree with and to those you do not agree with. Particularly important are your thoughts about ideas you disagree with— and what feelings then surface. If your disagreement is very intense, this might be a solid clue to a personal issue that may be getting in your way in business. If you can easily determine the issue, great. If not, don't worry about it. Eventually, you will be able to do so.

A Final Point

One of the most important parts of your breakthrough process is to learn not to always run to a so-called subject-matter expert to validate the truth of what you are being told, but rather to verify the information based on the results of what actually occurs when you act on what has been suggested. The same should be true for any other information that you are being provided in this book. Don't accept any ideas, suggestions or strategies as absolute truths until you can verify, in your own experience, whether they are correct. At some point you will develop a strategy for success that

works for you, and you will develop your own insights that work for you in addition to ones that you can offer to others who turn to you for help.

BREAKTHROUGH INSIGHT: Success comes from getting in touch with the part of you that knows how to succeed and then verifying this inner knowing with solid outward results or facts. When the results aren't favorable, or the facts don't line up, you need to re-think what you're doing or what you been told.

Summary

As we open up to the possibility of how emotional issues impact business progress, both positively and negatively, our ability to achieve predictable success increases. There's no reason we cannot learn how to work with our emotions in the same way that we learn any business process. The more we know about how we work emotionally, the more we're able to create productive directions. Saying emotions don't belong in business and, therefore, assuming they are not there is an absolute mistake, and a self-destructive illusion. Once we accept that business is often an outlet for, and directed by, emotional agendas, the road to success becomes easier.

Chapter 2

THE BASICS ABOUT BUSINESS EMOTIONS

The Powerful Role Emotions Play in Business

We're all driven in our personal lives, sometimes uncontrollably and irrationally, by our emotional needs. The same is true in our business lives, but most of us never realize it. If you're in business and you fail to see the powerful grip emotions, particularly destructive ones, have on everyone, including on yourself, lost income and opportunities are guaranteed.

Not yet convinced that emotional needs and agendas are played out in the business process? Stop for a moment and look around you. When emotional needs aren't met or are destructive, people quit jobs, kill business deals, miss deadlines, show up late, don't return phone calls, become argumentative, refuse overtime, renege on promises, dominate meetings, criticize others, talk too much…and the list goes on. Ringing any bells? Starting to see the stranglehold counterproductive feelings might have?

BREAKTHROUGH INSIGHT: The need for big money, power, attention, recognition and control, all acted out in the business process, are emotionally-based needs. Think about it.

If you've suffered financially or emotionally in business, it's time to take a new look at yourself and your business environment. And, if you want more for yourself and your family, accept the possibility that failure is totally dictated by misguided thoughts and feelings—yours and those of the people around you.

BREAKTHROUGH INSIGHT: When emotional agendas are in play, the financial success of businesses and the people involved is not always a top priority.

A Ground Floor Insight

If you find yourself continually losing to someone's political or other business tactics, you're not playing the business game correctly. Unfortunately, in business, the statement "Nice guys finish last" is often true, in a sense. It really should be "**Unaware guys finish last.**"

To succeed, you must learn to take care of yourself first and foremost—at all costs. And there's only one way to do that—have all true facts in any given situation fully in front of you, facts unblocked by emotional filtering or reformatting caused by incorrect beliefs about business and the people in it.

In the beginning, putting your absolute best interest first can be difficult, but not doing so cripples your ability to be who you truly are and get what you deserve. In fact, if the thought of having to honestly look at yourself or others so you can act in your own best interest is unsettling, this is a clue to misguided feelings and conditioned beliefs holding you back. Remember, you must accept the business world, and the people in it, as they are. There is no guaranteed way to change how people with emotional agendas blocking your progress think or feel. You can only change how you think and how you act in business. This is a hard truth for many of us, but, a life reality.

BREAKTHROUGH INSIGHT: Think of business as a card game. If you're in a card game and suspect someone is cheating, you have only two choices—get out of the game or play absolutely no-holds-barred to win. If you want to win, or even survive, in business and you can't do what's necessary, you have only one choice—come to terms with your "lot in business life."

The Challenge of Hidden Emotions

Identifying hidden emotional agendas, and acknowledging them, is hard and sometimes painful. In the beginning, this will take a persistent effort.

Here's your awareness challenge: Our destructive hidden, or unconscious, self is so clever it easily tricks our thinking so its agenda is followed. For example, it will orchestrate our thoughts so we believe we're protecting ourselves from possible disappointment. So, if you find yourself preparing for disappointment in something you are about to do, your hidden monster could be running the show. Consider closely what is happening. Mentally preparing for possible disappointment interferes with your ability to succeed. It creates stress, and stress limits creativity, a key to success.

BREAKTHROUGH INSIGHT: Being able to approach a business situation in a positive or constructive manner is impossible when destructive emotional issues are in play.

Why We Turn a Blind Eye to Destructive Emotional Issues

Facing the truth about destructive hidden feelings and agendas can be personally uncomfortable. In fact, it's sometimes even frightening, particularly when our financial security is at stake. Understandably, no one wants to believe that someone's irrational anxiety is creating a personal, let alone a business, problem. The reason is obvious: All of us know it's virtually impossible to deal with an irrational person…even when that person is one's self!

The party line in business that emotions have no place in business has a self-serving purpose—it keeps everyone comfortable by ignoring the unsettling reality that hard work, common sense and logic may not be enough for success. But if we ignore that as a possibility, we let emotionally destructive people sabotage our business well-being.

BREAKTHROUGH INSIGHT: When your life beliefs don't match something that is actually occurring, use that as a clue that you may be in the grip of an unconscious destructive agenda.

Still have doubts? Have you ever worked with someone who always criticized everyone and everything? Or ever been in a meeting where someone, let's call him Mr. Doomsday, finds endless reasons why a solid new business idea won't work? If so, was it apparent that his behavior killed motivation and creativity, even, possibly, to the point of bringing the business discussion to an absolute and frustrating halt? More importantly, did you wonder why he was allowed to continue to push his negative views? It may have been personally uncomfortable for anyone to openly challenge him. Or those in the meeting may have been afraid to push the idea forward notwithstanding

Mr. Doomsday's criticism because doing so may have put their jobs at risk if the idea failed. If Mr. Doomsday had a hand in it, you can bet it would fail, and any challenger would be blamed for opposing the advice of Mr. Doomsday.

Here's a quick insight: What's really going on with a Mr. Doomsday? Likely, he's anxiety-ridden and, in an unconscious way to cope with, say, his fear of failure, he attempts to control any business process he's involved in to manage his anxiety. So he constantly criticizes and tries to control everyone and everything around him toward that end. Unfortunately for others, this hurts the business process. Unfortunately for him, he damages his career.

One final point about why we may not challenge the destructive behavior of others. Doing so can force us to look at this possibility within ourselves. And having to acknowledge that we might unknowingly be holding ourselves back in the very same manner can be very disconcerting. It puts into question what we believe to be true about ourselves and the world around us, beliefs that we hold on to in an attempt to keep our anxieties and fears under control.

Mistaken Beliefs—Society's Failure Indoctrination

The most difficult challenges to business success are mistaken beliefs we've adopted based on what people told us at a time when we lacked the experience or expertise to objectively judge the validity of what we were being told. It is not unusual, for example, for well-meaning teachers, parents, leaders, or mentors to impose beliefs on us that they were indoctrinated with by their predecessors or ones they developed to cope with their fears, anxieties or other personal issues. These mistaken beliefs can distort reality and impair our ability to make effective decisions.

Unfortunately, many of these progress-hampering "truths" have been so deeply engraved in our unconsciousness that we no longer question them as reality. Removing them from the inner workings of our mind can be like moving a mountain. The difference in attempting to move a mountain is that the mountain is easier to see.

The Hans Christian Andersen story about the emperor's new clothes we heard when we were children embraced by our teachers and parents is a valuable, and possibly unconscious, message from the adult world. The emperor was told by two cheats who held themselves out as weavers that they could make him uncommonly beautiful clothes. The clothes, however, would be invisible to anyone who was stupid or not fit for office. The emperor was delighted and asked if they could make the clothes for him immediately. The cheats said they could. From time to time the emperor and his advisors arrived to watch the making of the clothes. When they could not see the clothes they were shown by the cheats, neither the emperor nor his advisors so commented because they felt their inability to see the clothes was due to their being either stupid or not fit for office. No one believed that the clothes didn't exist. It was only after the clothes were finished, during a royal procession to celebrate the emperor's new clothes, did everyone begin to see the truth when a startled child in the crowd shouted that the emperor was naked.

BREAKTHROUGH INSIGHT: It's not uncommon for a well-meaning parent to impose beliefs on a child that came from life illusions or other assumptions they developed to cope with personal anxieties or fears. The child invariably not only accepts these beliefs as true, but often never questions them in later life because they were ingrained before the child could properly assess the information. When these beliefs are counterproductive to life progress, they, in effect, create life illusions that block progress and happiness.

So, when you're struggling, you must take a hard look at everything you base your opinions and decisions on. That includes examining any assumptions that you have that may not be based on your own experience to ensure that a false assumption or two is not leading you down the wrong path, something I'll discuss in greater detail in later chapters. For example, if you're a woman and were brought up to believe that all men have an underhanded agenda, that belief can distort your relationships with men if you don't realize, and keep in perspective, that sweeping generalizations of this nature are foolish and self-limiting. Holding on to them can be nothing other than a coping mechanism that can distort your thinking without your even realizing it.

Now, let's see if we can develop the early indoctrination premise in the context of your own experience.

YOUR AWARENESS DEVELOPMENT SITUATION

Are you at times unhappy with how you react in certain situations? For example, if you can't carry on a lively conversation at a party, do you leave feeling dissatisfied with yourself? What about stumbling over your words when making an important presentation at a business meeting? Take a few minutes now, and see if you can identify some personal aspect that you're self-conscious about. No matter how small, write it in your Development Diary. If you can't identify any, place a mirror under your nose and see if any mist forms on the mirror to make sure that you are alive!

THE ANALYSIS

Let's assume you were lucky enough to identify a personal quirk that seems to plague you—one that you beat yourself emotionally about with no clue as to why—such as feeling awkward when talking to strangers at a party or something else that you feel self-conscious about. Did it ever occur to you that it could simply result from a lack of confidence based on your childhood experiences or some other unfair belief about yourself—an illusion that, for example, if you feel awkward when talking to strangers, no one is really interested in what you say or that people would think what you have to say might sound stupid? If so, can you recognize a masterful rationalization you've formed to justify why you hold on to this quirk, one that clearly absolves you from taking any responsibility for overcoming it? Can you recall someone in your life who may, in your mind, have been the cause of your quirk?

Bottom line: Criticizing yourself for things within you that were imposed when you were, in effect, defenseless will block your progress.

A Particular Risk for Would-Be Entrepreneurs

Irrational or mistaken life beliefs create a particular risk for people who dream of owning their own business. Sometimes these beliefs, as I've said, are deeply ingrained from childhood, and sometimes they are spontaneously developed as an excuse to avoid confronting irrational life fears. For example, people who want to start a business but are afraid of failing use a variety of illusions to avoid the fear of failing by coming up with rationale that justifies their not trying. By not trying, they avoid confronting their fear. For them, it's psychologically more comfortable to fail by not trying than risk failing by trying.

There is no doubt that inner conflicts and fears pop to the surface for all people in all new business ventures. But those successful entrepreneurs who are able to emotionally outdistance the typical business dreamers view the business process differently. Invariably, consciously or unconsciously, they know success is not predicting and achieving a particular goal, but rather a process of starting somewhere and ending with a satisfying result somewhere else, even if where they end up is not where they expected to be. Those who fail often have an irrational need to reach the goal they set at the start. That, for them, is their only benchmark of success. Very simply, steadfastly pursuing the initial goal in the face of problems—and there will always be problems—increases the risk of failure.

BREAKTHROUGH INSIGHT: People who are where they want to be in business intuitively understand that success comes through managing the roadblocks and wrong turns that are an inevitable part of the journey.

A point to consider: If you're a would-be entrepreneur and you find yourself endlessly mulling over what your chances of success will be based on pursuing a particular idea, this is a clue that you may be looking for a way out of starting your own business. Trying to factually determine what your chances of success might be is good—using market data and your own experience. But, that aside, trying to come to a conclusion (guess) about your chance of success can be nothing more than a mind game to make yourself comfortable—creating an illusion. If your underlying emotional makeup, however, is such that you cannot afford to lose, you might inadvertently make sure you do lose by devising a wonderful, face-saving rationale for not trying. Then you've lost. Sticking with the status quo allows little chance of finding opportunities.

BREAKTHROUGH INSIGHT: Some people rely on intuition in business. It is a useful tool. Without removing our emotional roadblocks, however, accessing our intuitive capabilities is difficult, because the intuitive course of action is blurred by our emotional needs, fears or conflicts. And then it's hard to determine whether our intuition or our emotional issues is steering us.

The Emotional Challenge is Different for Men and Women

As a general rule, men suppress their feelings far more than women do. They're uncomfortable dealing with displays of emotions and uncomfortable when they believe feelings are in play. So much so that some men aggressively criticize anything viewed as less than clear, unemotional thinking or behavior at every turn in the business process. The problem for them is that they easily and completely miss seeing when so-called rational thinking or behavior might in fact be based on counterproductive emotional needs.

Accessing and expressing feelings generally comes naturally for women, sometimes too easily and, sometimes for a few, uncontrollably. In many cases, their gut feelings about, say, a business idea or potential business partner can be extremely valuable. But, for them, this can create a dilemma, particularly around men who are absolutely convinced that feelings don't belong in the business process. So, the challenge for these women is to make sure they're not intimidated into ignoring or not expressing their gut feelings as a legitimate part of the business process. Feelings can be a valuable business tool, as long as they're expressed in a non-threatening way—which may for women mean wrapping them with so-called business rationale to keep the men around them calm.

Distorting Reality—A Major Risk

When our personal psychology distorts or blocks what's actually happening in business, we become factually blind. In effect, we develop emotional blind spots that cause us to miss destructive emotional agendas that move us in the wrong direction. We put a lid on our innate abilities. Our full business potential is never reached. On the other hand, if our psychological makeup is comfortable with success, there are few, if any, inner emotional agendas that will hamper our ability to succeed.

BREAKTHROUGH INSIGHT: What if, contrary to what you believed, you discovered that your boss or your spouse was dishonest? No doubt you'd be shocked. The hard truth is that our beliefs are often based on illusions that we have adopted to keep ourselves from being upset. Very simply, our psychological makeup dictates what we can handle, and if the result is self-limiting beliefs, we lose.

So what does this all mean for business? Simply, do not suppress, or run away from, your thoughts or feelings, no matter how uncomfortable it gets, even when they don't make sense. If you do, you miss the extent to which your, or someone else's, emotional issues may be supporting or interfering with your process or career.

Starting to Get In Touch — Handling a Difficult Person

If you suspect a business colleague is jeopardizing your ability to progress, trust the feeling, but don't react immediately. Take your time, and be alert to concrete indications, clues, which may support your feeling, something I'll talk more about in Chapter 6. Above all in this process, don't take anything that is said or done personally. If you do, and you react defensively or angrily, you'll block your ability to handle him or her effectively.

BREAKTHROUGH INSIGHT: Always keep in mind that a destructive person's agenda has nothing to do with who you are as a person or with your talents or capabilities. It's merely his way of furthering his own emotional needs, needs that are unlikely to benefit you.

So, just to get your thinking started about how to handle difficult people who you suspect may have destructive or roadblocking agendas, here are some basic suggestions:

- **Don't Fall Into Their Trap.** Never forget, emotionally destructive people are experts in making sure their agenda is fostered. Invariably, their strategy is to lure you into a provocative trap so you react openly. And if you do, since they know how to handle, say, a direct attack on issues or agendas that cannot be proven, they will make you look like you've lost your marbles. Their power often comes from the fact that most people are in denial over what is happening. They instinctively know their would-be victims search to make sense out of confusing situations, rather than open up to the possibility that their emotional craziness is in play. These skillful operators, certainly on an unconscious level, know and use that fact to their advantage.
- **Calmly Point Out the Facts.** Always calmly point out the facts about what is actually occurring. Don't try to get a colleague you suspect is manipulating a situation to admit that he has a hidden agenda, or that he is out to hold you back and take your opportunities. For example, if you need project advice and are not getting it from your boss, and you suspect that he is intentionally undermining you, don't tell him you suspect he wants you to fail. Instead, say something such as, "I don't seem to be getting any confirmation from you about the pros and cons of the project I am working on. Am I misreading this?"

Successful People Sense Right Action

Unfortunately, not a single business person is free from success meddling and unconscious feelings and thoughts—theirs and those of the people around them. Successful people, however, handle them better than others. They sense what they need to do, even when they don't understand the emotional dynamics.

Setting a Right Frame of Mind for Yourself

If you suspect that you might be getting in your own way or you are not where you want to be in business, here are a few starter suggestions about what to do.

- **Acknowledge You Are in Control.** Acknowledge that you are fully in control over your business destiny.
- **Acknowledge the Possibility of Personal Blind Spots.** Be open to the very distinct possibility that you may have emotional blind spots that are creating progress roadblocks.
- **Know You Can Eliminate Your Roadblocks.** Never doubt for a moment that, with persistence, you can push past any destructive emotional roadblocks, conscious or unconscious.
- **Don't Accept the Responsibility for Creating Your Roadblocks.** Accept the fact that any emotional roadblocks are the result of your honest reaction to what you were told as a child, or when you were otherwise impressionable. Or because of something within your personal psychology that you did not realize was creating a problem. By accepting them as not of your own making, instead of turning a blind eye to their existence to avoid feeling responsible, you can eliminate or manage them.
- **Don't Try to Change Anyone Else.** Never believe that you can change anyone else. Hoping to do that is a waste of time and a denial of the real issues. You can only change yourself. So, if you're struggling, there is only one person that you need to change—YOU. And that means changing the beliefs that you have about yourself or how the business world operates that cripple your progress.
- **Don't Believe You Don't Have the Talent.** Don't fall into the trap of believing that you are not where you want to be because of some innate inability.

With these suggestions in mind, don't miss a moment to uncover roadblocking emotional agendas within yourself. Your willingness to see what may be uncomfortable within you will unlock the hold any emotional roadblocks might have. When you glimpse the possibility of a roadblock and acknowledge it without guilt, your chances of overcoming it are dramatically improved. If, however, this becomes a struggle at any point, just openly acknowledge that your inability to look at the issue interfering with your progress is, in and of itself, a clue that the self-destructive part of you wants to hold you back.

BREAKTHROUGH INSIGHT: There will be situations when what you must do may not be personally comfortable, but, if you act properly, there will never be situations when what you must do will not be in your best interest.

Here's a challenge: The next time you meet someone who is totally preoccupied with making millions of dollars or climbing the corporate ladder, engage with him and listen carefully, particularly if doing so makes you anxious or otherwise uncomfortable. Move past your need to get away from him. Pay full attention to what he is saying. See if you can read between the lines and recognize how he may be struggling, for example, to overcome feelings of inadequacy.

Moving Forward—Your Awareness Journey

As I've suggested, when our emotional makeup allows us to accept success, we immediately, and sometimes unconsciously, move in a direction which increases our chances of success. On the other hand, when our emotional makeup does not allow us to accept success, we fail.

Now let's begin the process of enhancing your sensitivity to underlying emotional issues in business. To do this, it's not necessary to understand the psychological factors which may underlie emotional issues in a business situation. In fact, at times trying to figure out why, for example, we work for an offensive boss or why someone runs a particular company poorly may actually prevent us from dealing fully with the reality of what we have encountered and taking corrective actions. It's the old story—if you focus on the details, you will lose sight of the big picture. Once you are more aware of the feelings that surface within you, you will be more alert to the possibility of similar or other feelings in others you deal with. This can be of immeasurable help in getting the cooperation of others when you need them to assist your progress.

Toward this end, work through the following hypothetical business situation, a job interview. Put yourself completely into the imaginary situation. See if you can relate to the level of the job you are applying for while not forgetting where you are in your career. For example, if you are now a regional manager for a large company, try to imagine how you would feel if applying for a lower level job because circumstances required you to do so.

As you are reading the following situation, take a moment at the end of each paragraph, close your eyes and pay attention to all thoughts running through your mind and feelings you're experiencing. It's highly recommended, to accelerate your development, that you write your thoughts and feelings down in your Development Diary as the situation unfolds. Even those you don't think are relevant to the situation or are "business" related should be noted. For example, you might think of something you forgot to do yesterday. This in and of itself can be a clue to something within you that may be unknowingly getting in your way. To develop your new awareness, this is all the direction you need at this stage.

YOUR AWARENESS DEVELOPMENT SITUATION

You are going to be visiting Ramit Garage Door Corporation for an initial job interview as a trainee typing clerk. The company is eight years old, has seventy-three employees, and is run by its founder and president, Ralph Ramit. Ralph is twenty-seven years old and is supposed to be a boy wonder. You are told by the employment agency that Ralph Ramit takes personal pride in getting to know all employees.

Imagine that you have arrived at the appointed time, nine o'clock a.m., and are buzzed in through the front door security system. Walking in, you find yourself in the waiting room/secretarial work area. There is one guest chair piled high with boxes. Looking around the room, you see four cluttered secretarial desks and little space for anything else.

You are immediately acknowledged by a very friendly receptionist, Sidney, whose desk is loaded with file folders and little stationery-store knickknacks. Sidney apologizes for not having anywhere for you to sit in the reception area and shows you to an empty file room where there is a chair. As you take your coat off and sit down, Sidney leaves to tell Mr. Ramit that you have arrived. Within a few minutes Ralph bounds into the room, gives you a big smile, and asks you come into his office. As he is leading you down the hallway, he mentions that he got in at six thirty a.m. and is having a hectic day already. You notice Ralph is wearing worn green corduroy jeans and what appear to be leather rain boots.

Once you are in his office, he motions for you to sit in one of two chairs in front of his desk. He walks around his desk and sits in a high-backed, red velvet chair. As he sits down, he tells you that he likes a family-like environment to work in and usually prefers to hire people that he has known for years. At this point, Sidney walks in to ask Ralph, who is addressed by his first name, who should handle a customer on the telephone who can't figure out how to operate his Ramit garage-door control unit. Ralph, after a big sigh followed immediately by a slight smirk, picks up the telephone and talks the customer through the operating procedure. As soon as Ralph hangs up, the Ramit sales manager comes in and asks if it's okay to put a small weekly ad in the industry trade paper. He tells Ralph that it is a bargain rate. It will only cost thirty-nine dollars per month. Ralph says it is fine with him.

Ralph turns to you, apologizes for the ten-minute interruption and then proceeds for forty-five minutes to tell you about how he built the company into a $25,000,000-a-year business. This year, he explains, revenues will be flat because new home construction is at a low due to the current recession.

After his monologue, Ralph states he is impressed with you and asks that you fill out the Ramit employment application. As an aside, he tells you he designed the form himself one evening in only thirty minutes. He asks you to send the application in to his attention tomorrow. Ralph then stands up, thanks you for coming in, and hurriedly shows you out through the service entrance.

THE ANALYSIS

The simplest way to be more aware of your emotional undercurrents is to practice getting in immediate touch with all your thoughts and feelings in any given situation, regardless of what they are. This exercise was designed with that single purpose in mind.

Let's now explore some issues which may have been raised in this exercise. If you did not have any reaction to a particular issue addressed below, take a moment to identify any thoughts or feelings you have about the issue as you are reading the analysis. Try to recall if there were any momentary thoughts or feelings that you did not fully acknowledge. Remember this is not a test; it is only for your awareness development. There are no right or wrong answers. There is no correct number of issues which you should have reacted to. You can be equally successful whether you had only one distinct reaction or ten reactions. You can also be successful if you had no reaction. The important thing at this stage is simply to get the hang of seeing how you work emotionally in a business setting.

A Job Interview. Did the idea of having to go on a job interview prompt any feelings? If so, what were they? Did you, for example, experience any sense of anxiety? If you are very uncomfortable about the interview process, you may have consciously or unconsciously edited out acknowledging any feelings. Whatever the experience, take a moment now to think a little more fully about what you felt or didn't feel. Always keep in mind that it does not matter how you think or feel about yourself in relation to any issue raised. It is only important to learn to be fully aware of all your thoughts and feelings.

Company Business Identification. Did you have any reaction to Ramit Garage Door Corporation being in the garage-door business? If so, did you have any thoughts about whether it would be interesting or not interesting to be in that business? How do you think you would feel about telling your friends that you were in such a business?

Job Level. How did you feel about the fact that you were applying for a clerk-typist trainee job? If you are well along in your career, were you able to identify at all with that type of position? If so, what did you think? If you skipped over this aspect, you may have unconsciously edited out dealing with the issue. This is perfectly okay. If you did, knowing that you did so may give you some insight into how your unconscious emotional mechanisms work. If you are just starting your career, you still may have reacted to applying for a trainee position.

The Cluttered Work Environment. Did you have any thoughts about the fact that the office was cluttered? Would it normally make you think a company was poorly run? Did you have other thoughts or feelings, good or bad?

The Boss's Clothes or Name. Did you have any reaction to the way Ralph Ramit was dressed or to his name? How would you feel about working for an executive who dresses in an unconventional manner? What would your feelings be if everyone dressed in business casual in your office and, while a friend of yours was visiting you at your office, your boss came in wearing Bermuda shorts? Would you make an excuse for the way he dressed?

A Family-Like Environment. Did you like the fact that the president of a company was treated so informally by his receptionist? Would you have any reaction to a company president who wanted to run the business in a family-like way, including being involved in everyone's personal problems? What about the fact that Ralph liked to hire only people that he knew?

A Task-Juggler Boss. Did you have any thoughts or feelings about a company president who would be juggling a number of tasks while interviewing you? Would you think it rude or would you overlook it because he was the boss?

Okay, you should be getting the idea. Many other issues could have arisen in your mind when reading through this situation. For example, you may have reacted to the receptionist's being very friendly, to the cluttered receptionist's desk, to knickknacks being on the receptionist's desk, to the absence of a guest chair to sit in, to being asked to wait in an empty file room, or to the small reception/secretarial work area. You may have also responded to Ralph's big smile when he came in to greet you, to Ralph's having arrived at six thirty a.m., to his apparently wearing leather rain boots, to the type or the red color of Ralph's chair, or to the fact that his chair was covered in velvet. Perhaps you reacted to what appeared to be little spending discretion given to the sales manager. Ralph's directly handling a relatively small customer problem may have raised some issues in your mind. Did you experience any reaction to the company's flat earnings or to Ralph's saying it was due to the recession? What about the fact that Ralph designed the company employment-history form, that it was done by him late one evening, or that he gave you only one day to return the form may have provoked reactions? Did it occur to you that Ralph did not ask you about yourself, or that he hurriedly showed you out through a service entrance? Incidentally, was the receptionist a man or woman? Why did you make the assumption of male or female, if you did?

Once again, the point of this exercise is not to determine how many issues you react to, but merely to have you see how in any given situation any number of false assumptions, illusions or emotional issues could surface, particularly issues that jar your expectations of how business should be or that cause you discomfort. Typically, we consider many of these above issues minor ones, if we even acknowledge them at all. But they can offer clues to complex and underlying emotions which can cloud our business perception or thinking process. Acknowledging them is the key to uncovering their influence in our efforts for success.

BREAKTHROUGH INSIGHT: Thoughts and feelings caused by destructive or self-limiting underlying emotional issues can be much like static on a radio station. When there is static you cannot fully appreciate the program. The same is true when these types of thoughts and feelings flood your mind—your ability to clearly assess the situation and find necessary solutions is blocked.

As you begin to pay attention to your emotional undercurrents, you will find it easier and easier to identify roadblocks. Do not be discouraged if you found it difficult to identify thoughts or feelings in the Ramit situation. In fact, don't worry if you drew an absolute blank! By the end of the book, you will be right on top of your emotional process. You will be able to bring your emotional undercurrents into your conscious awareness.

Summary

Emotions play a powerful and sometimes hidden role in the business process. They dictate success or failure, both yours and those of people you work with. Facing this as a possibility allows you to gain control over your business progress. Assuming that emotions are not a critical component of the business process guarantees problems. Never forget that failing to acknowledge how and when emotions can sidetrack the business process is not of our own conscious making, nor the fault of those in business before us. If, from childhood, we have been taught to believe by well-meaning parents, teachers or mentors that something is true, we often accept it without further thought. Remember what people thought about the surface of the world before Christopher Columbus set sail for America? So, it's easy to see how our own life conditioning can prevent us from seeing what we should see to be able to move forward or resolve problems.

Chapter 3

GETTING COMFORTABLE WITH BEING UNCOMFORTABLE

The Comfort Zone Challenge

At times we perceive things in a way that makes us comfortable, but, in fact, prevents us from achieving success. When that happens, we're blind to the reality that we need to face to find a real solution.

To illustrate this point, consider the issue of world peace and ask yourself why have we not been able for centuries to achieve it? One answer, as uncomfortable as the reality would be, may be that it doesn't fit within overriding objectives by people in power. That they, for example, may have an unwavering need to dominate or crush others who have different beliefs. It seems ridiculous to think that people want killing and turmoil to continue, but it may be a reality. Can we say that we personally want peace but many others don't? That may also be a reality.

To expand on what could be a comfort zone issue blocking progress, assume for a moment that world peace was not achievable because the unconscious personal needs of the leaders make them emotionally incapable of cooperating. With that as an assumption, we might free our minds creatively to come up with the next best solution to our well-being on this planet. And that is the point. If you can look honestly at what may be a possible reality getting in the way in any problem situation, including your emotional needs, you're more likely to be able to make constructive adjustments. Unfortunately, the thought that there may be no basis for world peace is so unsettling that we choose not to accept it even as a possibility. We need to believe it is totally possible, even though history tells us differently. And that inability to entertain a possible reality may be the very reason we don't make some progress in making the world safer for everyone.

Let's take this concept personally one step further. What if you thought for a moment there was something within you that was actually the cause of all business problems that you have, and that any lack of progress was not the fault, for example, of someone else or just your own "bad luck?" Most of us are reluctant to fully accept that we might be the primary cause of our own problems in business, and, in fact, even in our personal lives. Clearly, that could push us up against the limits of our emotional comfort zone. The amazing fact is that if we did discover we were the primary cause, we would have the best chance of correcting our situation. We can always do something about correcting ourselves. We can rarely do anything to correct others.

BREAKTHROUGH INSIGHT: Always trying to change others to get what we need can be a clue to an underlying emotional roadblock. If you find yourself saying "If I could only get John to …", then you may be running away from an inner roadblock that prevents you from making progress.

The Consequences of Choosing Comfort Over Reality

We're led astray when our primary goal is to stay emotionally comfortable. Invariably, when we start to feel emotionally uncomfortable, our unconscious thinking reflex takes control and deceptively and masterfully repackages the cause of our discomfort into something we can live with. For example, when friends seem to be lying to us, our anxiety control mechanism jumps into action and we're likely to consciously or unconsciously rationalize, filter or reformat what we think is happening so we're comfortable—for example, rationalizing that we must have misunderstood. And if our repackaging process is finely honed, any discomfort will be fleeting.

So, to begin to identify your inner roadblocks, you must question the basis of your rationalizations. Let's say you found out that a co-worker always cheats on his spouse on business trips. How you feel about his behavior can be a clue to your own needs or illusions. If you rationalize away anything generally negative about the person's character, it could be because it suits your emotional purposes. And that can be a clue to something, unless honestly addressed no matter how uncomfortable, which could be an emotional blind spot that could impede your progress.

QUICK AWARENESS EXERCISE

Stop for a moment and think about your reaction to the cheating spouse example or the possibility that world peace might not in fact be achievable. Be honest with yourself. Get in touch with your reaction—don't judge it. One of the challenges in becoming emotionally aware is to grab those fleeting thoughts that slip by unexamined. Those are the ones that often surface from our need to be emotionally comfortable...not from our need to do the best for ourselves in life.

Let's dig a little deeper into how your comfort control mechanism might take over. If you were aware of the fact that President Clinton was caught cheating on his wife, Hillary, how did you feel when you found out? Did you buy into the political rhetoric and separate his personal life from his job standards? If so, you may have been rationalizing the reality of his behavior for your personal comfort.

BREAKTHROUGH INSIGHT: The key to making major progress awareness breakthroughs is to accept, without guilt, how you feel and think. This lessens the risk of creating false beliefs that roadblock progress.

Although it's difficult to hypothesize why any one particular person would rationalize inappropriate or hurtful behavior, we often do this because the truth is too uncomfortable or disappointing to see. In the case of President Clinton, it may have been that well-grounded people understood the human condition, were forgiving and simply looked for a cosmetic and palatable way to deal with it. In any event, the point is simply that, in uncovering inner roadblocks to your progress, the truth of what may have occurred is not as important as how you react to what occurred.

So, for example, if you catch someone lying or cheating and find yourself coming up with rationalizations as to why the particular act does not affect your well-being, or you say to yourself 'I want to look for the good in the person,' you could be limiting your ability to take care of yourself. Rationalizations can distort your ability to see when you're being taken advantage of because you're busily avoiding the truth. And this can cause you to miss opportunities.

BREAKTHROUGH INSIGHT: Your strategy in business should be to look for good people to work with, not struggle to find what's good in marginal people.

Another great example of people who innocently and inadvertently block their progress is those who chronically judge themselves unfairly. Nothing they do is ever good enough. And nothing they have is ever good enough. What never occurs to them is that doing this is merely their way of staying in their emotional comfort zone, at the expense of their happiness and success. Ever met someone like this? Undoubtedly, you have. Interestingly, it's easy to see it in others but not in ourselves—for reasons you should now understand. And if this describes you, just know that it could be an unconscious way you block fears and other uncomfortable feelings that might surface if you felt better about yourself. And, ultimately, doing this holds you back.

QUICK AWARENESS DEVELOPMENT TASK

The next time you talk to someone who obviously does something well, say a hard worker or a good parent, compliment him and pay attention to your immediate impressions if he looks uncomfortable.

QUICK ANALYSIS

People who can't cope with doing well constantly put themselves down. Compliments rattle their view of themselves—it moves them out of their comfort zone.

It's not uncommon, for example, for a man to hold himself back to avoid outdoing his father. Compliments push him against his need to believe differently.

The same can be true for beautiful women who feel they're not attractive. If you've ever-meet one, no doubt it was hard to imagine why she felt that way. If so, what you may not have realized was that feeling unattractive kept her emotionally comfortable. Simply, it was more comfortable feeling unattractive than dealing with feelings that would surface if she felt beautiful. If, for example, she struggled in her relationships with men, by acknowledging her beauty she could no longer use her belief that she was unattractive as the reason her male relationships failed. And she would then have to face what could be a far more upsetting reality about her—such as being afraid of men.

BREAKTHROUGH INSIGHT: Success comes from being able to re-examine what we think our business world reality is and to accept people for who they are, not from looking at the business world, and the people in it, in a way that makes us comfortable.

Laying Some Groundwork

Unfortunately, to stay in our emotional comfort zone, our view of how things should be is often based on how we want the world around us to be, not on what in fact it is. And that holds us back. So what should we do? Set the mental stage by laying the groundwork for honestly facing potentially uncomfortable awarenesses. And the best way to do that is to actively suspend our judgments and rationalizations about ourselves, the people around us and the world of business until the facts justify them. This may not be easy to do at first, but it's a key to reprogramming for success.

So, when something makes you uncomfortable, stay with the discomfort and avoid jumping to conclusions. Don't indulge yourself in rationalizations. Be patient. Relax. Watch for reality to surface—it will, as long as you don't push yourself to quell your confusion and anxieties. Eventually, you'll come to understand how judgments, rationalizations and unfounded beliefs keep you comfortable but block progress by filtering out what is actually in front of you. So, have faith in this process and look for ways to verify all of this from your own personal experiences.

BREAKTHROUGH INSIGHT: A clever way our destructive inner self keeps us from moving forward is by forcing us into compulsively overanalyzing upsetting situations—a form of mind static. If you have a problem with someone, for example, and find yourself spending hours, days and even weeks mulling over that person's motivations, that's your clue that you may be roadblocking an awareness that you need to come up with an effective resolution. The reality is you'll never know the person's real motivations unless, of course, he tells you—and, even then, it may not be the truth. By wasting time actively cluttering your mind with hypothetical assumptions, you block clarity.

Another Try at Yourself

Let's work through another exercise to explore your emotional side in a hypothetical business situation. Try to relate to how you would feel if you were the person in the story. Once again, close your eyes from time to time as thoughts emerge so you can fully connect with them. Make every effort to write all your immediate thoughts and feelings down as you read through the situation, particularly ones that feel unsettling or create subtle conflicts. Do not read the analysis discussion until you have explored all your thoughts and feelings.

YOUR AWARENESS DEVELOPMENT SITUATION

Assume you are a professional salesperson. You went through a bitter divorce about a year ago and have not socialized since. It has been a lonely and depressing time for you. Within the last several weeks, you moved to a new town to take a job with a company that manufactures photographic equipment. You recently made a sales call on the purchasing manager for a prospective customer. The company you called on could be a major new account. The purchasing manager was a warm, down-to-earth, and attractive person. You were told by the purchasing manager at the end of the meeting that the company would like to place a $1,000,000 order for your company's equipment. You were also told to call to confirm the details of the order in two weeks. When you called, the receptionist informed you that the purchasing manager was on vacation but that the purchasing manager left word you could call any evening. The receptionist gave you the purchasing manager's home number. You called one evening and, after discussing the order, learned the purchasing manager was also recently divorced. You know that your company does not approve of its employees dating customer employees. Possible personal problems in such a situation could risk potential future business.

THE ANALYSIS

This is the type of situation in which a person's personal needs may affect his or her business life.

Let's explore a few thought possibilities. Did you have any thoughts about the purchasing manager being warm, down-to-earth, and attractive? Does warmth equate to non-professionalism or weakness in business in your estimation? If you are a man, do you think a businesswoman would have the same reaction as you did to this question? If you are a woman, what do you think a male's response would be to this question? Do you think your response to how a member of the opposite sex would react is influenced by any particular past dealings or involvements? Did you have any reaction to the thought of being a salesperson?

If you were so inclined, would you have asked the purchasing manager directly for a date? Or would you just let it be known that you may be receptive to going out and wait for the purchasing manager to make the first move? It would not be unusual for someone who was very lonely to overlook any risk of losing his or her job by pursuing a customer socially. Do you have any rules for yourself or people you work with about dating customer employees? If so, where did they come from?

Were you aware of making any judgments about your particular reactions to any issue? Were you anxious or concerned over any of your thoughts? Did you attempt to push any of them out of your mind? If so, and you are using your Development Diary, make note of them in your Diary.

The actual reactions or thoughts you have are not important. There is no good or bad response. It is only important that you see what your reactions or thoughts are and you learn to dig deeply for them. If you had little or no thoughts to the various issues raised, it is also important to be aware of your lack of reaction. You may be pushing thoughts out of your conscious awareness.

Emotional Blind Spots

When we don't see reality in front of us, we are, in effect, emotionally blind. For example, when what someone does or says makes no sense, no doubt you've run into a reality blind spot. If it weren't for the blind spot, chances are good the situation would make sense, but not in the way you'd like to think. The fact is, as I've suggested, that we have difficulty seeing reality when it doesn't conform to what we were told it should be or what we want it to be. Blind spots alter the reality in front of us to keep us comfortable at the expense of finding solutions to issues that hold us back.

Blind spots are a particular challenge because, as I've also suggested, they're often ingrained deep into our unconsciousness when we were children or young adults, passed along by fears and misguided beliefs and illusions adopted by well-meaning parents, teachers and mentors. Add to these any self-destructive ones adopted to avoid our fears or bad feelings, and our chances for making the best possible business progress are reduced—dramatically.

So, if you've ever felt anxious, uncomfortable or confused in a business setting but didn't understand why, chances are good you bumped against an emotional blind spot. A part of you recognized something that was upsetting or confusing, but your comfort zone control mechanism short-circuited what was happening before it consciously surfaced and put you into an emotional dead end.

What's the answer? Identifying and eliminating emotional blind spots is, of course, the obvious solution. But to do that you first must understand the cause, and that may not be possible without professional help. The good news is that understanding what might cause blind spots is not necessary for progress. But here's the challenge: Your unconscious inner monster will fight tooth and nail for its "reality" belief survival over your true well-being. Anything that challenges the beliefs that, in effect, manage your fears and anxieties is viewed as a mortal threat by your inner monster. And it wants to stay in control regardless of the cost to your true well-being. But, if this might be true for you, with some basic insights into your life patterns and beliefs which I will explore, you can manage yourself as you would manage an unruly child and break the code to your unwitting destructive behavior.

BREAKTHROUGH INSIGHT: A destructive inner self can be so powerfully creative that it can convince us, through our rational mind, that there is really something we should run from by instantly repackaging what is in front of us in a way that makes us comfortable. Finding freedom from a destructive inner self is difficult. In effect we have to murder a part of who we are. The "life" of a destructive inner self depends on staying in hiding—the source of its power. Taking charge over a destructive inner self requires you to constantly re-think what you believe if you're not moving forward.

Here's an example of what happens when we inadvertently adopt beliefs that distort reality. Many believe that people are basically honest. And that's commendable. But, all too often, it's a classic life illusion used to keep them emotionally comfortable. How about you? Any reaction to the suggestion that people may not be basically honest? If you're not comfortable with this possibility, you may have an emotional blind spot. And, if you believe people are basically honest, ask yourself, where did your belief come from? Take a moment and think about it.

I'm not suggesting that the belief is right or wrong. I'm only suggesting that there is no way to know whether the belief is generally true. It's an assumption not based on hard facts. In effect, it is an illusion. In fact, we can't possibly know whether a particular person is trustworthy other than through dealings that confirm that belief. And, even then, we may be misled.

Still not convinced? Consider this. We listen to news broadcasts every day that describe event after event in which people are lying, cheating, stealing and abusing others for personal gain. Who are these people? Are they from another planet? Are we to believe that people in business are in another category? Not if you want to prosper. Blindly believing otherwise to keep your inner fears under control puts you at risk—you're less likely to spot people out to take your money or pounce on your career or business opportunities. By the same token, there's no need to generally believe people are untrustworthy. So, what should your strategy be? Simply, don't form an opinion about a person's honesty until you see how the person acts over time. This won't be easy to do at first—you'll have to learn to live with the anxiety of not knowing, something most of us have a great deal of difficulty doing. But, if you can withhold forming premature opinions, you won't be misled. And, as with this or any other general belief, when you form a belief before you know all the facts, never doubt for a moment that your inner destructive monster is working overtime to reformat what is in front of you to keep you emotionally comfortable.

BREAKTHROUGH INSIGHT: People who lie, cheat and steal in business have a distinct edge. They know we think everyone is generally honest, and, while we're asleep at the wheel, so to speak, they smoothly and cleverly go about maneuvering us for their personal advantage. They know that if we question their veracity, they have a good chance of convincing us otherwise because it's upsetting to see distasteful possibilities.

When you're able to squarely face things that might make you cringe, you will not distort reality about yourself or the world around you. And when you confront reality, it's less likely that emotional roadblocks embedded in your psyche will lead you down the wrong path. For example, consider this: Do you sometimes feel you really have no aptitude for business and will never amount to anything, or a similar putdown thought? If so, stop for a moment, live with the momentary discomfort and see if you can identify someone who may have instilled that unfair thought, such as a parent or teacher, in your mind. If you were able to do so, consider yourself very lucky. You may have found the source of your problem, something in the back of your mind that you believe is true because you were told it when you didn't have the experience to properly evaluate it. And then you'll have something to work with to gain a better perspective on a belief that is not well-founded.

TWO AWARENESS DEVELOPMENT EXERCISES

Exercise One

An interesting way to gain insight into how your subconscious self works in preventing upsetting feelings from surfacing is to identify one anxiety-related issue that is constantly on your mind. For example, that pay raise, promotion or job you're worried about. If one doesn't come quickly to mind, keep notes of various concerns you experience during a business day. You might be surprised to find one you lived with so long you don't even realize it's always present.

Once you identify a recurring anxiety, make a note of it on paper and attempt not to worry about that issue for one day only. Try to keep it completely out of your mind or, if you can't do that, don't dwell on it when it pops into your awareness. This may be hard at first for a variety of reasons. It may be, for example, your negativity is in high gear, causing you to struggle with what you believe to be inevitable disappointment. Make notes during the day of any anxious thoughts that pop into your mind, in effect mind static that can block clear thinking and progress. This will help sensitize you to how you unknowingly may be getting in your own way.

Exercise Two

Another way to increase your awareness of how your emotions get in the way of your progress is to pay attention to how you react to an upsetting business situation. Take a moment now and think about what you typically do when facing a business disappointment, such as not getting the raise you hoped for or being beaten out by a rival for the position you wanted. Collect your thoughts on paper—doing so brings them into sharp focus. For example, do you go to a quiet place by yourself and think, or do you rush into a distracting activity, one that helps you forget what happened? Do you feel worthless, or do you take the disappointment in stride and look for another strategy to get what you need?

After collecting your thoughts, consider the following. When you're too hard on yourself and do not fully acknowledge and manage unforgiving feelings, you hold yourself back. And, when you face disappointment, if your opinion about yourself is particularly low, you may compound the problem by acting out angrily or otherwise doing something that ultimately is not in your best interest.

Exercise Objective

The point of these two exercises is to start uncovering thoughts you may have paid little attention to in the past that could hamper clear thinking. By diligently tracking your thoughts, you'll gain valuable insights about yourself for future use and help you identify thinking patterns that could interfere with your progress.

Failure as a Way to Stay Comfortable

Has anyone in business told you flat out that his goal was to fail? Undoubtedly, no one has. The sorry truth, however, is that to stay emotionally comfortable, failure becomes the unconscious goal of many people. In their case, success unmasks feelings that are more troublesome than not reaching their potential, particularly when they can rationalize that achieving success is something not within their control. So, in effect, staying comfortable means choosing a state of being that is the least troublesome for them.

Although those that do themselves in to stay emotionally comfortable seem to follow many different routes, what's interesting is that when you take a hard look at what they're doing it becomes clear that there is a basic destructive behavior pattern. This pattern is often missed because self-destructive behavior defies rational thinking.

Here's a classic. Ever met someone who just made it to the top, and then did something so seemingly out of character, or so obviously dumb, that he destroyed everything he worked for? Like the newly elevated corporate manager who suddenly starts drinking heavily at lunch and ends up getting fired? If so, you've seen self-destructive behavior, first hand. And inevitably you've met someone whose unconscious goal was to fail in order to stay emotionally comfortable.

BREAKTHROUGH INSIGHT: The reasons that failure agendas take control are sometimes so emotionally complex that only years of therapy can loosen their destructive hold. But, no matter how complex the cause, their drivers are always the same and always simple—to stay emotionally comfortable, no matter the cost to career, business or family.

Self-destructive behavior is clearly unnerving to witness in others. As I've said, it forces us to consider that possibility within ourselves and those around us on whom we may depend. But by accepting it as a possibility in ourselves and in others, we have a fighting chance of clearing any success roadblocks. So, if you're not where you want to be in business after years of trying, step up and embrace the uncomfortable possibility that you may have unconscious emotional agendas doing you in. Doing this will be your success jumping-off point.

BREAKTHROUGH INSIGHT: When we glimpse unsettling possibilities within ourselves, our so-called rational mind jumps into action and blocks or twists the awareness into something we can emotionally accept. We're particularly susceptible to this reformatting when dealing with people we depend on.

Positive Thinking—A Reality Check on a Classic Belief

One of the first steps in reformatting your thinking for business to increase your effectiveness is to identify the various business myths, or illusions, that block progress or send you in the wrong direction. This is something I'll be spending a lot more time on in later chapters. There is, however, a classic belief worth mentioning now: To get what you want in business all you have to do is to think positively.

Most of us, certainly in our early years in business, connect with this logical, seemingly easy to do suggestion—think positively and your goals will be achieved. And why not? After all, it's easy to see that you can't succeed if you think negatively.

Here's your first reality check: Have you ever tried to maintain a positive attitude? If you have and you found that it's easy, consider yourself very fortunate. No doubt, you have and will continue to be very productive in your business endeavors. On the other hand, if maintaining a positive attitude is something you struggle with, then clearly you have not reached your potential, nor are you using your full talents.

The reality for most of us is that even when we think positively, we still struggle to reach our goals—or, we should say, the goals we tell the world, and even ourselves, we want to reach. When that occurs, the irony is that we easily become negative about thinking positively! "Why should we believe that a positive attitude works? Look what just happened!" we say to ourselves. And, then, it's even harder to think positively—often causing us to give up trying and lapse into old negative thinking patterns.

The real question then is: If positive thinking is the magic success bullet, why doesn't it always work? The answer is simple, but not obvious. Our thinking is contaminated with underlying, and generally unconscious, self-destructive and self-limiting thoughts and rationalizations. These are thoughts that unconsciously keep our personal anxieties under control, but which in fact prevent us from truly prospering. A familiar theme?

People with compulsive behaviors are a good example of what happens when underlying emotional conflicts drive thoughts and behavior. By compulsively acting or thinking in a particular way, they're able to relieve, or at least lessen, irrational anxieties. Their thinking and behavior, however, often prevents them from relating well to people and prospering. In effect, they manage their underlying personal anxieties through their compulsiveness, leaving them with an anxiety they can live with—emotional pain and even failure in business and in their personal lives.

BREAKTHROUGH INSIGHT: If you're not where you want to be in business, do you often think the problem is caused by something out of your control, such as bad luck or poor timing? If so, never forget that thoughts such as these are great examples of how your destructive unconscious mind delivers rationale to your conscious mind that, so to speak, takes you off the responsibility hook.

Here's your second reality check: If you must force or continually remind yourself to think positively, that is a clue that you've been overtaken by an inner destructive agenda. And then you must consciously dig deep to see if you can identify when you may be acting destructively. If, for example, people don't seem to be responding well to what you're saying, don't blame them. Look inward—openly and honestly. Only then do you have a chance of eliminating any underlying cause blocking your progress or, if you can't identify the underlying cause, at least developing a strategy to work around it—something considerable time will be spent on in later chapters.

BREAKTHROUGH INSIGHT: Having to push ourselves continuously to think positively is like putting a fresh coat of paint on a rusty car body—we have not solved the problem. And doing this is a clue to an inner agenda that's not serving our true best interest. Very simply, actively having to think positively will not, by itself, overcome the control unconscious and destructive emotions have over us.

QUICK DEVELOPMENT TASK

Stop for a moment right now and see if you have any fleeting thoughts or feelings….disbelief about what was just stated, a feeling of helplessness or? If so, make a note in your Development Diary so you can keep track of these and similar thoughts and feelings. Over time, you may see a negative pattern that you are completely unaware of. If you do, this awareness will help set the stage for ways to unblock your progress.

So, in a nutshell, positive thinking is not the answer for progress. No doubt it supports any efforts toward progress, but it only works when destructive emotional agendas are not controlling thoughts or actions. So, what's the solution? Allowing our innately positive nature to surface by acknowledging, and eliminating or end-running our hidden destructive emotions. One great way to do that is to simply stop thinking negatively. That, of course, if negative thoughts run roughshod over you from time to time, can be challenging. But a great way to start is to re-train any negative thinking patterns by consciously dismissing any negative thought onset immediately.

BREAKTHROUGH INSIGHT: When you have a negative thought, immediately say the word "cancel!" Over time, if you track your thoughts and feelings in your Development Diary, you'll find, probably much to your surprise, that you'll become more positive in your attitude and in your approaches. Don't worry about whether you identified the inner feelings that may be causing this. Simply canceling the negative thought will move you forward. In fact, what's interesting is that underlying destructive agendas may fall away without your knowing it as you block the symptoms of their existence as they surface

---

Summary

Getting comfortable with being emotionally uncomfortable is your first hurdle in identifying and managing for success emotional roadblocks that interfere with your progress, and that includes identifying and managing emotional blind spots and personally unverified beliefs that can lead you astray. Over time you'll discover that the discomfort you may have always been avoiding is in fact something that, if you sit with it for a while, you can manage. And if you learn to always live with any momentary emotional discomfort, you will find that your ability to progress will increase.

Chapter 4

SLEIGHT-OF-HAND DECISION MAKING

The Business Lie

Here's the dirty little business secret: Business people often make decisions that satisfy personal needs first, then justify them with plausible business rationale. When these needs are at odds with business goals, business suffers. And so do they. As you now know, this invariably happens without the decision maker, and even those affected by the decision, realizing it.

Unfortunately, the path for covering up non-productive emotionally-based decisions is greased because the business community is in lock-step denial about facing the crippling business reality proposed at the start of this book: All business decisions are driven by emotional needs—those that are good for business and those that are bad for business. In fairness, however, it's easy to see why there is complicit denial by the business community. After all, how comfortable would you feel facing the possibility that your career or business progress was dependent on someone else's irrational emotional agenda?

So, it's understandable, in a sense, why the business community's mantra is that emotions should not be a part of the business decision-making process. The inadvertent conclusion is that, in virtually all cases, they aren't. Couple this with the fact that business schools and the business community add fuel to the fire by providing a wealth of easily accepted rationale to cover up emotional agendas, and it becomes obvious why the reality of what drives the decision-making process is pushed aside. The real shame is that failure to address the emotional component is the very reason people and businesses struggle year after year to find the magic success formula and why, in reality, business is more like a game of lotto than the pragmatic success process everyone would like to believe.

BREAKTHROUGH INSIGHT: The true enemy to productive business decisions is the belief that emotions must not be a factor in the business process, and, therefore, they are assumed not to be present. It's easy to tell someone that he must stop at a red light and expect that to happen. It's not easy to tell someone that emotional needs he is totally unaware of must not be a part of his decision-making process and expect that to happen.

The Cover-Up Challenge

When a business decision is driven by emotional or purely personal needs, the decision maker invariably finds, consciously or unconsciously, a logical dollars and cents basis to justify it for reasons that are obvious. Can you imagine the response if a company president stood before her Board of Directors and asked for a $200 million headquarter relocation to cut her daily commute by thirty minutes? Nonetheless, the same corporate executive with the same motivation might carefully lay out a plan, in a very impressive relocation report, showing the business benefits of moving to a newer building. The move, then, would appear to be strategic, rather than personally motivated.

Decisions based on counterproductive personal agendas are more likely when the decision maker is not fully in touch with his real emotional needs. And, as you now know, if the needs are counter to good business judgment, failure is inevitable. For example, a corporate executive may fully believe that the new corporate headquarters he has proposed is in his company's best interest, even though he may momentarily think he would feel better being in a larger office, or in one with a water view. In fact, thoughts such as these may be the driving force behind the entire expenditure.

The real challenge is identifying when personal issues are distorting the business decision-making process. A corporate executive presenting a plan to open an office in China may not be totally, and quite honestly, aware of the control his personal inclinations have in his decision-making process. He may fully believe that doing this would be in his company's best interest. The only thought flitting through his mind might be how nice it would be to be able to visit China and explore its culture. And that, in fact, may be the driving force behind the decision. On the other hand, he may feel that his personal needs should top any business needs, and any decision that meets his personal agenda is perfectly acceptable.

For some people, decisions that serve personal needs are first and foremost. The narcissist and the sociopath are classics. If you are involved with one, you may not catch on for years, if ever. These folks instinctively know how to manipulate others in ways most of us would never think of to get what they want for themselves. They have us at a real disadvantage. When we're following what we think are rules of fair play, they're plotting how to use these rules against us. They're fully aware that most of us want to believe everyone is playing fairly by the same rules. But, for them, all of this is a game. When they cheat, for example, they count on no one else to cheat. Hard to believe? Write your thoughts down in your Development Diary. If you find this possibility unsettling, that could be the very reason that you don't see what is really happening.

As suggested earlier, typically, in what otherwise can be an upsetting, even, at times, frightening, world around us, we unconsciously adopt a set of beliefs that keep us in our comfort zone. And when these beliefs are not well-founded, our psychological makeup causes us to filter what we see and hear so we remain emotionally comfortable. If staying comfortable is your goal, you can be led astray, especially by the smiling sociopath and the glad-handing narcissist.

BREAKTHROUGH INSIGHT: A clue that you may be filtering reality to keep anxiety levels down is when you are struggling in your career. When we struggle, meeting one seeming roadblock after another, invariably there are only two things getting in our way—our life beliefs and our counterproductive emotional needs.

Let's take a moment and examine how emotional needs might steer you into a decision that is not necessarily in your business best interest—which will also help you understand how others may do the same.

YOUR AWARENESS DEVELOPMENT SITUATION

Assume you are a purchasing agent for a large electronics manufacturing company, and were just told to purchase a computer system to implement needed inventory controls. You must choose between two competing systems. One system, System A, is made by the world's leading computer manufacturer, Company A. The second system, System B, is made by a less prominent manufacturer, Company B. Company A has supplied eighty percent of the data processing equipment your company now uses. The new purchase must be approved by the president of your company, John Methebest. John, although very outgoing and socially conscious, has absolutely no technical background. John hobnobs with other top company executives and never misses an opportunity to boast that his company uses only the best. Your immediate boss had been responsible for the purchase of all your existing Company A computers. The choice between the two systems is to be entirely up to you. In fact, your boss and the president gave you this project because, in your last job review, the only negative your boss listed was an apparent inability to assume the responsibility for making decisions on your own, something both he and the president felt would hamper your chances of promotion.

After researching the systems' capabilities and running tests, you determine there is a distinct chance, because the function to be performed by the computer system is completely novel, that neither system will be fully capable of doing the job required. System B is clearly technically superior. It will process work thirty percent faster than System A, likely saving hundreds of thousands of dollars each year, and stands the best chance of doing what will be required. Since you did the analysis, no one else knows System B is technically the best.

You don't have to provide the technical backup for your decision. The president and your boss will accept your verbal recommendation of which system should be purchased. You know if you pick System A and something goes wrong, it's likely that Company A would be blamed. On the other hand, if you pick System B and something does not work as planned, you might be blamed for selecting a computer built by a company that is not a market front-runner. In fact, there's little doubt in such a situation that the president would say you should have selected System A because Company A is the world's leading computer manufacturer. In a nutshell, if you choose System A, chances are excellent that you will not be blamed for any technical problems that arise. And no one will ever know that it is not as efficient or as cost effective as System B. What would your choice be?

Take a moment before reading further to write down your thoughts and feelings in your Development Diary.

THE ANALYSIS

The purpose of this exercise, again, is to help you bring into full focus the basis of all your decisions—business and personal. Being unaware of the emotional aspects of your decision-making process can easily limit your capabilities. The point is not to judge what you would do, but to see what you do based on what you think and feel. This, at times, may not be in the business best interest of the company you're involved with.

If you chose the personally safe route and selected System A, your decision may be based primarily on an emotional need to avoid career risk. You would not be alone in doing so. If you made the safest career choice in this more obvious situation, you may unknowingly take the same emotional approach in areas less clear-cut to you. One more question: If you took the safe way out, do you think you would have been mad at your boss or the president for not "letting" you make the best profit-oriented business decision? Take a moment and think about this.

A suggestion for the future: The next time you face a business decision, write your considerations down. After doing so, take a moment and ask yourself the following questions:

Did you find yourself making the safest personal choice rather than one which is the best dollars-and-cents business choice?

If so:

- To what extent are you inclined to cover it up with solid business rationale?
- Are you uncomfortable having to cover up personal needs, such as risk avoidance inclinations?
- Do you feel your progress is limited if you cannot take reasonable business chances?
- Do you think your management is limiting you in any manner, or could it be that, for example, you purposely joined a company that does not encourage business initiative?
- If not, how do you now feel about your business decision process? Pretty good, we hope!

BREAKTHROUGH INSIGHT: In approaching life in business, don't kid yourself about any statement that a particular decision is a bottom-line, dollars-and-cents decision, either on your part or on the part of others. Emotional factors are ever-present in the business process. There's nothing wrong with that. There's nothing we can do about it. But if you acknowledge this as true, you won't unknowingly limit yourself or be misled. And you will free your thinking so you are able to get the most out of your abilities.

Coping with Business Unknowns

The business process is filled with unknowns. Unknowns bring to the surface irrational fears, anxieties and even painful personal issues. As a result, business decisions are often based on illusions or other unfounded assumptions adopted to cope with business unknowns, illusions and assumptions that soothe our mind by keeping us emotionally comfortable, but ones that self-destructively clog our business judgment. When that happens, the decisions create undue risk.

Here's an example. People working for large companies often speculate endlessly on their career path to eliminate unknowns. They assess and reassess their future depending on changing corporate circumstances. If the picture looks favorable one day, they're happy. If the next day it doesn't, they're unhappy. Day-to-day their happiness depends on what they think will happen, an illusion, not necessarily on what actually happens. These obsessive speculators ignore the facts. Some, for example, start looking for a new job if they think their company is starting to experience financial problems. It doesn't matter that their company has historically weathered many financial uncertainties. What's interesting in these situations is that these folks usually have little, if any, financial or business background needed to effectively evaluate their company's situation. Nor do they typically have access to meaningful data to make solid determination of the company's viability. Once their anxiety takes over, reality is irrelevant. The only issue that takes center stage is finding what they believe to be a secure job. Invariably, the need to be anxiety-free trumps true business judgment, so much so that they may not even take a close look at the situation they are moving into. Finding a new job to relieve anxiety becomes more important than the actual job found.

BREAKTHROUGH INSIGHT: If you're working for a financially troubled company, consider the real possibility, as part of your stay-or-go analysis, that as people begin to bail out of their jobs, higher-level jobs can open up rapidly. By sticking with the company you may in fact have an unusual opportunity for advancement if the company turns itself around.

What about you? Were you ever unhappy with your business progress? If so, did you feel you'd be happy if you reached a certain career goal? If you reached that goal, were you satisfied? Or did you eventually feel empty after your goal was achieved? If so, did you set another goal and stay focused almost daily on it? There is nothing wrong with goal setting for the right reasons. In fact, goal setting is extremely useful in making progress. But if the reason for the next goal is merely to run away from issues that otherwise would take you out of your comfort zone, such as not knowing the future, then you could be limiting yourself. Your issue may simply be coping with the anxiety that is created by not knowing what will happen. Not honestly recognizing why we are really pursuing a course of action can easily lead to poor business choices. When emotions take over, business sense takes a back seat.

YOUR AWARENESS DEVELOPMENT SITUATION

Let's try the career path guessing game. Assume you're a senior sales executive for ControlRight Company and that you were passed over last month for the position as president. You just received two outside job offers from two prestigious companies as the second in command. One offer is from Columbia Corporation, whose president is 63 years old. The other offer is from First Time Corporation, whose president is 47 years old. The president of Columbia is paid an annual salary of $350,000. The president of First Time makes $425,000 a year. The job offer from Columbia is at an annual salary of $120,000 and the job offer from First Time is at an annual salary of $95,000. Without considering anything else, which job would you take and why? Write your thoughts down in your Diary before going further.

THE ANALYSIS

Now that you've recorded your thoughts, let's look at the situation. There are many possibilities—none are right or wrong for the purpose of this exercise. What's important is that you see the way you deal with this situation, to give yourself some insight into how important **what you think will happen is in making a business decision.**

Consider the following questions and write your answers in your Diary, if you did not do so already:

- Would the job offer from Columbia be the one you would lean toward? If so, why? If not, why?

- Do you think that a situation in which the president would retire in a few years would probably give you a chance at the top more quickly? Or would money be the issue under consideration?
- Would you be willing to take less money for a chance at possibly more money later, or would you feel you should take the most you could get as soon as you could get it? If so, would you possibly be less concerned about advancement?
- How would you feel about taking a job which pays much more but has little chance of advancement? In such a situation, how would you feel if your boss were ten years younger than you?
- If you would take the higher paying job at Columbia and felt there was no chance of getting the top job, would you feel good or bad about it? Why?
- If you would take the lower paying job at First Time, would you have any anxiety thoughts surrounding that decision? Would you think it just your luck that the spot wouldn't open up at the top, or if it did, you probably wouldn't get it?
- How would feel if you took the job at Columbia and the president, after you had worked there for two years, was given a five-year extension on the mandatory retirement policy by the Board of Directors?
    - Would you think it had anything to do with your abilities, that if you had been better, the Board would not have extended his term?
    - What would you now feel about your chances for the top job?
    - Would you think that you had five years before you had a shot at the top? If so, why?
    - If the president were having health problems, how would you feel?
    - What would you think about the possibility that the Columbia president would quit before the end of five years? Why? (Did you just catch yourself thinking negatively?)
    - Would your thinking be different if you heard a rumor that a new director who seemed opposed to the existing Columbia president had just been elected to the Board? Why?
    - Did you feel tense as you were considering these questions? If so, can you pinpoint what the tension is related to?

These questions merely address some of the many issues which could create evaluation concerns for you. If you related to any of them, you have some insight into how you operate—how you decide what to do based on valid and invalid assumptions. Always keep in mind that assumptions, or illusions, may arise from past experiences, what others told you or your underlying fears. When that is the case, it should now be easy to see how layers of assumptions can cause you to arrive at decisions that are not unemotional, bottom-line business decisions.

One final point: Trying to figure out all the possibilities in any given situation, deciding what the most likely results will be, and then basing a decision on these conclusions is a good business approach. But when doing so, you must identify when you're working overtime to predict outcomes based upon illusions or unfounded assumptions arising from underlying emotional needs or concerns that you're not acknowledging, illusions and assumptions that can impede your business progress. By recognizing when emotional issues are involved and then factoring them into your analysis process, you're more likely to make solid business decisions and less likely to act to satisfy needs that could ultimately be detrimental.

At times we create illusions when we're anxious about what we think will happen to avoid feeling that we can't do anything more than sit tight until the events or people allow us to move forward. For example, have you ever tried to get someone to do something, such as go into business with you, and then had to wait for him to make a decision about whether he wanted to? Did you spend time trying to figure out if he would commit to going along with you? If so, you likely felt good if you thought the answer would be "yes" and bad if you thought the answer would be "no."

The next time you're trying to assess the outcome of someone's decision, see if you can let go of having to think about what the answer may be. Just accept that you won't know until the person actually tells you. If you don't spend time trying to determine an answer, you'll be free to implement more constructive directions and strategies. In fact, a good business and emotional approach in these types of situations is to spend your waiting time developing another business possibility. This way you have plans for all possible outcomes. The alternative possibility may in fact turn out better than the original one. For many people, however, a second option can create anxiety if they're not in touch with their roadblocking emotional needs. When faced with two good possibilities, these people become confused about which choice is best. For them it's better to avoid potential anxiety by not finding alternatives, rather than to increase their business success chances.

The point is to always deal with issues if and when they occur, and avoid making decisions based on what may occur. Simply, avoid limiting yourself now because you don't think you would know what to do if faced with something else that may surface.

Interestingly, a real, as opposed to an imagined, choice is never as difficult to make as we guess it would be. In fact, when presented with the facts, very often the decision path becomes obvious. The key, then, is to recognize the anxiety created by our emotionally-based illusions or unfounded assumptions about how we imagine we would think or feel. So, in your awareness process when decision situations create anxiety for you, don't be hard on yourself. It's more important to recognize what is happening than to try to relieve your anxiety or feeling of guilt about how you work. Eventually, all of this will come automatically and you will have clarity.

BREAKTHROUGH INSIGHT: Learning to deal with reality, not overindulging yourself with "what ifs" is the key to success.

What does all this really mean? It means giving up control to the unknown, something people often have a hard time doing. And yet the unknown always has to be acknowledged in any business situation. Those business people able to do this are often given a wide-open career track. They seem to be able to predict how others will act or how situations will turn out better than most people. Do you wonder what they have? Well, invariably they're not as inwardly conflicted as others. They see things as they really are. So, once you see things as they really are, it's much simpler to gauge what outcomes may be in given situations. How we perceive people and circumstances is based upon our emotional eyesight. Perceiving anything in a manner that keeps anxiety at a minimum can put you in trouble.

BREAKTHROUGH INSIGHT: Trying to predict outcomes is often only an exercise to calm ourselves down.

Fear —The Number One Reason for Sleight-of-Hand Decisions

Fear, whatever the basis, is the top cause of sleight-of-hand decisions—decisions that really address emotional issues, not business progress. This happens in Corporate America all the time. Employees block progress day in and day out based on fear—fear of the unknown, fear of being fired, fear of not meeting their business goals, fear of not being accepted, fear of not getting a raise. And the list goes on. Fear often surfaces as negativity. Being thought of as negative clearly rings some discomfort bells, but being told you have no guts can be worse, especially if you're a male. Whatever the cause, fear is the biggest business hot button, even for those who always appear optimistic.

Accepting the *possibility t*hat fears could be driving our decisions allows us to deal with fear constructively. Not doing so blocks our ability to effectively manage fears that clog progress.

Managing our fears can be a real challenge. The next time you're starting to worry, sit down with your Development Diary in a quiet place. See if you can identify what you think may be at least one underlying cause. Write it down, no matter how ridiculous or unrelated it seems. Do this each time you start to worry, and you'll begin to see your fears as you should, an excuse to avoid issues that no longer have a place in your life. Once you understand that, you will have another powerful tool to use in moving forward in business.

Learning to manage fear is critical because business problems often make us confront our deepest fears, such as not being financially secure. Interestingly, there are always people who enthusiastically attack business obstacles. Problems to them are personal challenges. They go forward constructively, even though they may experience moments of self-doubt. They've learned to live with their fears. And that allows them to cope with outcome uncertainties and overcome emotional impediments created by feelings that cause others to give up rather than risk failing.

The trick to dealing with fears when facing problems is to constructively find opportunity-creating solutions and not simply run away from the challenge to relieve anxieties. All too often the anxiety of not immediately knowing a solution cripples us. We see this in our personal lives every day. It's easier to get a divorce than learn how to cope with a "difficult" marriage partner, including one's self! There's no personal growth unless you learn how to welcome and solve problems calmly and keep your anxieties under wrap. Giving up based upon what we think we can't do because we're afraid we can't is guaranteed failure.

BREAKTHROUGH INSIGHT: The way you emotionally react to issues in business can be the sole reason you believe there is a problem.

Summary

The real basis for business decisions is rarely acknowledged. The fact is that business people all too often make decisions driven by irrational or unproductive emotional needs. They then spend time and money justifying these decisions with what appear to be plausible business rationales, not only to the detriment of their company, but to themselves as well. To be successful, you must be able to separate personal and emotional issues from true profit-oriented issues in the business decision-making process. Otherwise, you risk failure.

Chapter 5

SETTING AN EMOTIONAL FRAME OF REFERENCE

Waiting to Find Out Why Is a Mistake

There are almost as many theories about why people have particular emotional issues that get in their way as there are therapists to treat them. So, attempting to discuss general theories of why we have or hold on to emotional eccentricities is of little value in getting us on the best possible track.

While it's not impossible to identify emotional issues blocking your progress, believing you can identify any not in your conscious awareness on your own is a major challenge. And, even if you can, eliminating their destructive hold on you, depending on how deeply ingrained they are, can take, at best, months of counseling.

So, what can you do on your own? Simply learn to become aware of how you function emotionally in the business environment, and then learn to develop strategies that end-run progress blocks. And, as you learn to end-run them, many will simply drop away. All of this is eminently possible, if you have the desire, with the awarenesses and techniques in this book.

Don't Blame Someone Else

A major stumbling block to success is not taking full responsibility for your own progress. How many times have you blamed your parents for dumping some emotional "hang up" on you that you feel is holding you back? By the same token, how many times have you been aware enough to see that they were in the same spot as you were? They had unfair emotional issues dumped on them before they knew what was happening. Should you then blame your grandparents? Where does it stop? A parent with an emotional hang-up is no different than a parent with a genetic problem. It will undoubtedly be passed on to his or her child. The child will pass it on to his or her children. Sometimes the labels change, but the results are always the same—unhappiness in one form or another. What sometimes changes is our method of covering up the underlying issues.

By the same token, don't blame your mentors, teachers, or even your significant other for imposing limitations or other roadblocks on you that slow you down. Clearly, it was unintentional—at least in most, if not all, cases. Those who may have set you on the wrong path or otherwise contributed to your lack of progress are undoubtedly working with blind spots and emotional limitations that cloud their thinking. It is your responsibility to identify when an imposed roadblock or limitation is getting in your way and to do something about it yourself, which does not mean trying to reframe the thinking or beliefs of others to make you feel comfortable. It means accepting what has happened and eliminating or end-running these imposed progress blocks, something I'll continue to explore for you as you read on.

Don't Blame Yourself

Now this is going to seem to contradict what I just told you, but if you harbor feelings that your lack of progress is entirely your fault, you can self-destructively trap yourself. The reality is, as suggested earlier, that before we even knew what was happening, the seeds of our unconscious roadblocks and distorted beliefs were firmly planted in our minds. And often the unfortunate result is a lifetime of unsuccessfully trying to move ourselves forward.

Now, couple this with the fact that we're told by experts in human emotions that figuring out our hidden inner conflicts and roadblocking issues is very complex and can take years of therapy. That may be true. But accepting these conflicts and issues often stops us dead in our tracks—or puts us on a progress and life hold indefinitely. This is not to say that emotional health professionals are not an extremely valuable recourse. They are. And, in some case, they are the only answer. But believing that resolving deep-seated emotional conflicts that block progress is complex can be a deterrent to finding a way to move ourselves forward. Experts often focus on details and miss the obvious. And if people think something is too hard to understand, they give up without trying.

Here's the real issue: Most of us, even experts, don't look for simple solutions. But when great solutions are found, have you noticed they're often simple? Does it take a genius to find a simple solution? Most of us think so. But in many cases that's not true. The "genius" who saw something the world missed was often less distracted by conventional thinking and therefore free to see the problem clearly. This is, in effect, what you are being asked to do in this book—to re-think how you view the business process from an emotional point of view. That will allow you to find simple solutions to any business roadblocks, regardless of what, up to now, has held you back.

So, in a nutshell, let go of feeling responsible for your personal roadblocks. This will allow you to develop. Punishing yourself for things that you didn't create is a losing game.

Now, let's see if together we can develop our premise of re-positioning our thinking to clear emotional blocks in the context of your own experience.

YOUR AWARENESS DEVELOPMENT SITUATION

Take a few minutes now and see if you can identify some personal aspect you find troublesome, an emotional conflict that causes you to react in a way you're uncomfortable with. For example, if you cannot carry on a lively conversation at a friend's party, do you leave feeling dissatisfied with yourself? How about stumbling over your words when making an important presentation at a business meeting? No matter how small, write it in your Development Diary. If you can't identify anything, place a mirror under your nose and see if any mist forms on the mirror. If none forms, no doubt that you are free from emotional issues which the rest of us poor souls must endure.

THE ANALYSIS

Let's assume that you were lucky enough to identify an upsetting emotional hang-up you think you have. If so:

- Is this something that you've been frustrated about for a long time?
- Do you feel this is how you are, and you're stuck with it? Like being shy, awkward or unlucky?
- When you think about the issue, are you self-critical? Do you feel your conflict is preventing you from real success?
- Do you blame someone in particular for your being the way you are or just yourself?
- What about any other conclusions you've reached about yourself that, in effect, might be a rationale for not trying to reach your goals?

If any of this might be true for you, have you accepted your lot in life—that your dreams will never be realized? If so, now seriously consider whether in fact the conflicts are of your own making or the result of something, for example, you were told as a child. Again, the key at this stage is to see how you work emotionally.

Inner conflicts often pop to the surface when we are developing new approaches or ideas, such as when starting new business ventures or making career changes. Yet when we examine situations in which business people have outdistanced others, we find new concepts or directions have been pursued. They had no established criteria for determining their chances of success. Most of us might think that would be a disadvantage. In fact, it can be an advantage. Without preconceived notions, we're more open to seeing opportunities as they develop. Digging into our past experience to decide whether something will work is valuable. If our emotional makeup, however, is such that we cannot afford to lose, we might inadvertently make sure we do not lose by not trying. Then we've lost for certain. Sticking with the status quo allows little chance of finding opportunities. But starting something, anything, offers great potential for discovering opportunities. They may not be what we expect, but that is how real success begins.

BREAKTHROUGH INSIGHT: Some people rely on intuition in business. It's a useful tool. Without removing our emotional roadblocks, however, accessing our intuitive capabilities is difficult. And even if we are able to access our intuitive capabilities, emotional conflicts often blur the results, making it hard to determine whether our intuition or conflicts are suggesting a course of action.

Your First Success Process Strategy

Success is not based on figuring out today what will happen tomorrow; it is based on *learning to identify when anticipated outcomes to present decisions are based upon illusions or unfounded assumptions arising from emotional conflicts or issues within ourselves.* Decision based on illusions or unfounded assumptions, such as fear-based or self-limiting thoughts, can self-destructively block your progress.

To help you put this concept into a working framework, let's explore ways you may be blocking yourself when confronted with new business directions by working through an awareness analysis process.

A SUCCESS PROCESS STRATEGY

The next time you're trying to decide whether to pursue a business direction, take the time to write in your Development Diary every thought that goes through your mind in your assessment process. Don't edit out any thoughts. If you judge yourself as you make your Diary entries, write down how you judged yourself. For example, if as you write you feel you should not think or act in a particular way, write that down. Make sure you put every thought down, whether or not you believe it's relevant.

If nothing comes into your mind, do not push yourself. Take a break and do something physical that requires little intellectual effort, such as riding a bike or taking a walk. Any form of physical activity will work. After an hour or so, go back to your writing and try again. If nothing seems to come, then write anything down, even if it consists of senseless sentences or a string of unrelated words, such as "John, like, pursue, blue, and I am not happy." Do not worry about sentence structure, spelling, or anything else. The point is just to begin writing words on paper. This will get you started.

After you have finished writing your thoughts, take at least a thirty-minute break before continuing. After the break, review what you have written and underline every thought that you think is based on or comes from an emotional source within yourself rather than based on absolute fact. Do not underline the thoughts that are based upon facts. For example, if your decision not to pursue a direction was because a prospective partner told you that he did not want to be involved, this should be considered a thought based on fact. That you did not choose to try to interest another partner may be emotionally based. If you're not sure whether the thought is based upon fact or not, underline it.

Now below your listing of all your thoughts, you'll be setting up two columns of information on your Diary page and any following pages you may need if your underlined thought listing is extensive. On the left side of the page write the category "UNDERLINED THOUGHT" and on the right side of the page opposite this category write your thought. Leave some space below the "UNDERLINED THOUGHT" category to add four additional categories: "THOUGHT SUMMARY", "UNDERLYING ISSUE", "FACT OR ILLUSION", AND "CHANGE OF CIRCUMSTANCE", as shown in the example below. Consider an assumption not based on hard fact to be an illusion.

Once you've finished, reduce all underlined thoughts to four words or less and write this summary on the right side of the Diary page opposite the "THOUGHT SUMMARY" category. Let's assume, for example, you wrote

"I decided not to pursue the idea of going into a retail business partnership with John because if the venture failed, my family would have to give up the lovely house we live in." You might restate this as a THOUGHT SUMMARY in your Diary as: "Loss of house." The restating is important because it will help you identify underlying emotional issues you do not readily see. Don't worry about whether you are correctly restating your original thought. That's not important. What is important is to begin the process of trying to identify underlying emotions and learning to separate fact from illusion.

Now see if you can extrapolate a related emotional feeling and write this on the right side of your Diary page opposite the "UNDERLYING ISSUE" category. For example, "Loss of house" may then relate to being embarrassed because it might in your mind indicate failure to your friends. If so, write "Embarrassment" on the right side of the page for this category.

Now, opposite the "FACT OR ILLUSION" category, list whether this aspect in your decision process, in this case "Loss of house" is based on a fact or an illusion. The house had not been lost, so this clearly is an assumption—an illusion.

Finally, opposite the category entitled 'CHANGE OF CIRCUMSTANCE", list what change or changes of circumstance could alter your decision to move you forward. In doing this, let your thoughts or ideas flow without judgment. Even if the ideas seem ridiculous, write them all in your Diary. In this example situation you may put "Find outside investor." This might give you adequate lead time to get your business successfully off the ground.

Your page for this process would look like this:

THOUGHTS

I decided not to pursue the idea of going into a retail business partnership with John because if the venture failed, my family would have to give up the lovely house we live in.

My wife was late for the train this morning.

My cash reserve is low.

UNDERLINED THOUGHT: I decided not to pursue the idea of going into a retail business partnership with John because if the venture failed, my family would have to give up the lovely

	house we live in
THOUGHT SUMMARY:	Loss of house
UNDERLYING ISSUE:	Embarrassment
FACT OR ILLUSION:	Illusion—loss of house
CHANGE OF CIRCUMSTANCE:	Find outside investor—lead time

When you've finished, put your Development Diary aside until the next day.

Get up early the next morning so you have time to review what you have written. At that time your mind is fresh. As you review what you wrote, see if any change of circumstance, even one that seemed ridiculous, farfetched or unattainable at first, can actually be made to happen. For example, assume you said that you would be emotionally comfortable if someone backed you with one million dollars, but you felt there was no way to get it. If you feel you cannot raise the money and have never tried, re-think why you don't think you could. Countless numbers of business people do just that all the time. For example, if this were the case, would you feel you can't because you do not feel anyone would make that kind of an investment in you? If so, instead of your making that decision, let a prospective investor tell you. In the process of trying to raise money, you may discover how to modify your approach to make it attractive to an investor. In looking for money, you may gain valuable experience or come up with another business idea better suited for the marketplace. You may discover how to increase your chances for raising money on your next idea, or you may learn what type of approach you need to take to get a business going for yourself. Just because you were not able to sell an idea of yours doesn't mean you didn't make progress. After thinking this through, seriously re-think how you might move yourself forward.

Making progress in business means learning how to evolve your approach. Too often people who get turned down on their first attempt just give up. If you didn't know how to play golf, would you consider yourself a failure at the game if your first game score was poor? Of course not. You would realize that it takes experience, knowledge, and practice to hone your playing skills. The same is true in business, yet people rarely pursue business in the same manner as they pursue, say, a new sport. The process for both, however, is the same.

Summary

Clearing your mental deck is critical to progress. There are a few basics you need to keep in mind that will help you push forward. First, if you discover that something within you is blocking progress, don't waste your time trying to figure out the cause if it's not readily apparent. That's something you can do as you move forward. And don't allow yourself to dwell on who you might think put you in the spot you're in or feel guilty for whatever impediments you've held onto—take the complete responsibility for getting yourself out of any predicament you're in.

Chapter 6

IDENTIFYING EMOTIONAL ROADBLOCKS

Spotting Emotional Baggage

Most of us bring into our adult life unconscious emotional baggage that blocks access to our full innate talents. When we're free of business-crippling emotional roadblocks, we do extremely well. When we're not, we pay an emotional and financial price. Very simply, unconscious roadblocks blind us to obvious ways to progress.

While it's upsetting to realize we're doing something wrong, it's even more upsetting to find out we're doing something we had no idea we were doing and, worse yet, not know what it is or what may be causing it. So, when we're not where we want to be in business, the challenge is figuring out if there is something unknown causing a problem—whether within ourselves or in someone else or a combination of both. Clearly, it's unrealistic to believe you could possibly uncover the cause of someone else's unconscious agenda. And it's likewise very problematic to believe that, without professional guidance, you could uncover the cause of your own unconscious agenda.

So, the real question is: How can you personally spot what you're unconsciously doing to cause a problem when you don't have a clue to what it could be? The key word is clue, in this case—the solution to finding progress.

A Multistep Process

Before getting to a discussion of how you can use clues to identify roadblocking agendas, it's important to keep in mind that clues alone are not the complete solution to progress. Making progress when underlying feelings may be in play in business is a multi-step process. Once you have possible clues, you need to kick-start a thinking and action process that ensures you'll avoid unknowingly repeating whatever got you to where you don't want to be. And that will require you, at a minimum, to let go of having to know why something is happening and just deal with the result of what is happening.

Clues, Discomfort and One More Strategy

There's no doubt that, when our progress seems to be on hold, looking for the cause and eliminating it is always preferable. Unfortunately, as I suggested, this may not always be possible and may be impossible when hidden emotional agendas are running the show. So, what do we do? Well, now you know: Look for clues.

Seeing clues to destructive emotional agendas takes effort at first. We filter most clues out of our awareness to stay emotionally comfortable. When you get the hang of it and realize that it may be your only hope for progress, however, you'll learn to work with them as you would with any other business tool.

There is no simple rule of thumb for determining whether a clue exists. All too often, clues are not what we would expect them to be. Some appear to be normal reactions to what may be going on. For example, how often do we see chronic complaining as a clue to underlying self-destructive inclinations? Or, for that matter, unsettled feelings, restlessness, anxiety, fear, boredom, unhappiness or feelings of inadequacy? Clues might also surface as provocative actions or statements, such as being late to meetings or being negative. Any of these can be tip-of-the-iceberg indications. As you become comfortable accepting the realities of what is happening around you, spotting clues to roadblocking agendas is something you'll become skilled at doing.

Once you have clues, your options will be to eliminate the cause of the hidden roadblock, which as suggested may not be possible, or develop strategies to end-run the roadblocks you can't eliminate—which can always be done. From your vantage point now, however, all of this may seem doubtful, but if you persist using the approaches and ideas discussed in this book, you'll be able to determine for yourself, from the results of your own experience, not only that they will work, but how well they will work.

BREAKTHROUGH INSIGHT: If at this early stage you doubt you'll be able to end-run personal roadblocks, use that as a solid clue that your destructive self is already engaged in shutting down ideas, solutions and approaches that can move you forward.

To be skilled at identifying clues, as stated in Chapter 3, you must be willing to live with the discomfort of seeing something destructive within yourself or those around you. And, as you learn to forgive yourself and others for having self-destructive tendencies, you'll become adept at consciously identifying clues to agenda roadblocks as part of your everyday reality.

Here's a hypothetical situation to work through to get you started thinking about how to end-run an emotional roadblock whose cause you can't identify or eliminate.

AN AWARENESS DEVELOPMENT EXERCISE

Assume that you're an entry-level manager who believes that success is being the president of a Fortune 500 company. You desperately want to succeed, but your performance ratings are poor, in spite of the fact that you've spent years trying to improve by reading books and taking management courses. You're completely frustrated at this point because you cannot seem to really get a handle on why you're doing poorly.

Stop for a moment before you read further and see what you think might possibly be a clue to an emotional roadblock in this situation.

Well, if you haven't guessed, don't worry—you'll catch on the more you work with the process. The clue is the fact that you have the desire but are unable to achieve the results you want.

At this point, now that you have a clue, you have several options. One is to spend years in counseling taking a hard look at possible psychological blocks to your progress. Another is to accept the distinct possibility that an unconscious aspect of yourself is setting you up for failure—and take the responsibility for doing something about it. For example, it may be that you're working for a boss who is threatened by you and is judging you unfairly and you've done nothing more than to complain about how he is holding you back. If so, you may find by being honest with yourself that you have little confidence that you can do well and that his treatment of you merely reflects how you feel about yourself. In any event, whatever the reason, acknowledge the possibility that you're being self-destructive by continuing in the relationship and accept the full responsibility for eliminating or end-running the roadblock.

Recognizing, in a situation like this, that you may be pursuing a self-destructive path as a distinct possibility is a key to setting your creative mind to work. And that will allow you to honestly explore thoughts that may signal, for example, that you really have no interest in being a top manager and are only doing it to please someone else. Or that you should start looking immediately for another job, taking a new management course, or begin exploring what you're naturally good at and then rethinking the way you have been approaching your business career. The point is to re-think how you've been thinking, and not just do something that might relieve anxiety but which won't move you forward.

A Personal Learning Experience

Working through roadblocks became all too clear to me during a consulting project. A major client called one afternoon and asked me to review a lengthy proposal he needed for a ten o'clock a.m. meeting the following day. I was jammed and asked one of my associates, Anthony, to jump in. Anthony was personable and good at what he did, but he was not always reliable when asked to work in the evening. His heavy social commitments sometimes took precedence over his business commitments. Since Anthony had been a longtime personal friend and experienced people like Anthony were difficult to find, I tolerated his sporadically unreliable work ethic.

In any event, as soon as the work request came in, I asked Anthony if he had time that evening to review the proposal for the client's morning call. Anthony said he had a dinner engagement, but would cut it short and work through the night if necessary to review the proposal. I specifically asked Anthony if he was absolutely sure he could do the work. He emphatically stated that he would get it done. In fact, he said he would have Marilyn, his secretary, come in at seven o'clock a.m. the next morning to start making any necessary revisions. Unfortunately, adding to the problem with Anthony, Anthony had a tendency to tell people what they wanted to hear.

The next day I arrived at the office at seven o'clock a.m. and, relieved, found Anthony at his desk furiously working away on his laptop. My relief was short-lived. When asked how it was going, Anthony sheepishly said he had just begun, needed five hours to finish and wanted someone to ask the client to delay his meeting. "You know those women," he said, "they never know when to let you go even when you tell them you are under pressure to get work out for a client!" He said by the time he got home, he was too tired to concentrate. Even with help, the job couldn't be completed by the deadline. The deadline was missed, and the client was very unhappy.

Let's examine what happened with Anthony from an emotional perspective. The consulting business frequently required late night efforts. Anthony had been asked to work from time to time to meet deadlines. Every once in a while, he did not complete the task he promised because of his social commitments. He couldn't discipline himself when he had female distractions. Obviously, confronting Anthony and getting an assurance from him to do the job was not the answer. He couldn't say no to anyone, including his female dinner companions. Because Anthony had a driving need to be liked, he always tried to accommodate others. The need to accommodate actually blinded Anthony to the consequences of making too many commitments. Anthony had an obvious emotional roadblock to his success in business. When it affected me, the problem became mine. By not factoring in Anthony's repeated behavior, I realized that the real roadblock was mine and not Anthony's—shown by the decision to use Anthony on a critical overnight deadline project.

As far as my situation with Anthony was concerned, I had an emotional roadblock. Even though I spent month after month complaining to myself and my wife about Anthony, I never did anything about it. I never saw the situation I put myself in. If I had been able to fully recognize and accept that Anthony would not fulfill his obligation to me, I could have avoided the last-minute crisis. My roadblock was that I did not want to see Anthony as he was because he was a personal friend. By acknowledging that Anthony would probably drop the ball again knowing he had a dinner engagement, I could have cleared my thinking to come up with a better strategy. But, instead, I insisted in my mind that Anthony should take responsibility for doing his job and that he should see that jeopardizing the client relationship would be foolish. I was kidding myself. My brand of logic had no place in this situation. I was dealing with an emotional roadblock—and ultimately it was mine, not Anthony's. For Anthony, his personal people-pleasing needs invariably overrode any other needs, including making a living.

YOUR AWARENESS DEVELOPMENT SITUATION

What would you do in a situation like the one involving Anthony? Have you ever been involved in a similar situation? If so, what did you do? If you've ever been involved in a similar situation and successfully solved it, draw now on what you've learned so far before reading the analysis. Jot your thoughts down in your Development Diary.

THE ANALYSIS

If your response to this type of business problem would typically be to complain continually to others about how unreliable Anthony was, you may be dealing with an emotional roadblock of your own. Complaining will not solve the problem. It's an excuse for not taking positive action or, in fact, for acting self-destructively. The Anthonys of this world rarely change.

Working With Clues

Clues can tell you many things about hidden destructive agendas. They can alert you to situations when you're creating illusions or false beliefs to cope with something that is difficult to emotionally process and to when someone else is doing the same.

One of the best examples of a clue to a roadblocking agenda worth mentioning now is when someone does or says something that makes no business sense, such as not letting anyone fully express opinions during a business meeting by constantly interrupting him. In these types of situations, rather than wasting time complaining about it or searching to make sense out of it, accept it and develop a strategy for handling it. Keep in mind if something like this happens to you when you're giving your opinion and you take it personally, that's a clue to a roadblock of your own.

BREAKTHROUGH INSIGHT: When people prevent others from expressing their opinions by cutting them off, what is really being interrupted, unknown to the interrupter, is the surfacing of uncomfortable feelings in the person doing the interrupting.

As I've suggested, many roadblock clues are easy to recognize, but we don't see them as clues to possible agendas we need to look at more closely. This, in part, may be because we don't realize the true underlying significance of what we or others are doing or saying or because we've been socialized to accept certain behavior or response patterns as normal and acceptable. A good example is the situation just discussed with Anthony. Anthony's behavior caused him to miss deadlines when his social life took a priority, something, up to this point, you may not have read as a clue to an underlying self-destructive inclination. We also miss clues when we have beliefs that we never question. For example, if you believe that emotions don't belong in business and assume, therefore, they're not present, you can easily miss seeing the possibility that, say, a decision, was an irrational, emotionally-based decision.

Making matters even more challenging is that we've been conditioned to accept our emotional side and the emotional side of others only within certain parameters. For example, it's completely acceptable to cry if you are a woman, but, generally, not if you're a man. On the other hand, it's generally not okay to be depressed once in a while whether you're a man or a woman. So, in effect, we accept crying within certain limits as good, but not depression. As with many generalizations, it's easy to accept either view as true in all cases. In some cases, however, depression, at least momentarily, may be therapeutic, and crying may signal something dangerous. In any event, either can signal a destructive underlying emotional issue that should not be dismissed.

BREAKTHROUGH INSIGHT: At times we become depressed when our conscious self is working overtime to keep a painful emotional issue from coming to the surface, which, if addressed, would no longer be an impediment. If depression is viewed as an opportunity to resolve a hidden issue, provided of course it's not chronic, it may be no more worrisome than crying

---

Common Clues to Look For

As I've stated, to increase your effectiveness in business, you have to identify when you or someone you're dealing with has a hidden emotional agenda that blocks progress. The simple way to do this is to look for clues. If you become skilled at catching your random thoughts, you'll find it's easy to spot clues, provided you can tolerate seeing the information in front of you. Trying to figure out the actual hidden agenda behind a clue is often impossible and a waste of time. So, as with any new awareness ideas, the easy way to start, as I've suggested, is to be open to the possibility of hidden agendas when, for example, your gut tells you something is amiss.

BREAKTHROUGH INSIGHT: You may find in the beginning that increasing your emotional awareness is easier said than done. Even considering the possibility that irrational agendas might be controlling the business process is an uncomfortable thought. But, if you don't persist in the face of discomfort, you will fall short—not only in business, but in your personal life as well.

Now, let's put what I've been talking about into the context of your business process and explore common clues to hidden agendas. The following clue listing is not all-encompassing. It's simply a sampling of obvious ones that may surface—and meant only to kick-start your thinking about clues to hidden agendas and needs, both in yourself and in others.

The behaviors or beliefs in the various clue categories may overlap, but are separately identified to trigger specific awarenesses. Worry and anxiety, for example, are listed as separate clues, but they can actually be different labels for the same thing.

Belief Illusions

We all get caught up in beliefs which we never question and which have no basis in fact—what I'll call belief illusions, which will include any assumption not based on hard fact. These are beliefs that we've unsuspectingly welcomed with open arms, such as beliefs we've had imposed on us when we were not in a position to question them or ones we've personally created to stay emotionally comfortable. Any one of them can put and keep us on the wrong track.

The ones that we've adopted to keep ourselves comfortable are clues to underlying, and often irrational, agendas that can distort reality. The ones imposed on us at a time we couldn't properly assess or challenge them—such as extreme political beliefs about the general motivations of a particular class of people—are equally dangerous to our progress. Virtually every one of them is based in emotional needs, fears or anxiety-ridden issues.

We're particularly susceptible to belief illusions when we're anxious about future outcomes. A great example of this is the reliance many people place on long-range and detailed business plans. Clearly, these plans set business objectives, which is good. They give everyone a solid starting focus. And they minimize risk anxieties by framing unknowns in ways that makes us comfortable. But, because of the difficulty many have in facing the unknown, business plans often take on a life of their own. They become future reality, the reality by which success is measured, particularly if it is filled with glorious financial projections. And these exciting revenue possibilities, at times, can cause us to suspend our common sense. The result is that they often serve as the unwavering road map for what to except—even when the evolving facts dictate otherwise. In effect, if we're not careful, they become belief illusions that can lead us astray. No one can predict the future, unless, of course, it's failure and we have a hand in it!

My first lesson in understanding the power of business plan illusions was brought home early in my business career. My partners and I decided to get a working capital loan to expand our consulting business. In our first bank meeting, the bank manager asked where our company would be in five years. I responded by saying that the only thing that I could verify was what the business had done in the past, that we planned to pursue every opportunity in our business area as we had done and that we were going to make every effort to meet or exceed our past growth rate. I added that there were so many variables in any business that no one could know with certainty how the future would play out. Clearly, this was not what the bank manager wanted to hear. The loan request was turned down. The following week, a five-year projection was put together and another bank was approached. When asked the same question, I simply handed the banker the five-year business projection, and said that it reflected what we intended to achieve. The loan was approved, and a valuable lesson was learned: Even though it's impossible to predict the future, at times, we need to indulge people in illusions to make them comfortable and to get what we need. Failing to recognize that relieving anxiety may be as important to the business process as coming up with solid business ideas can limit progress. And believing otherwise can be a clue to an emotional roadblock.

BREAKTHROUGH INSIGHT: Virtually every day, we manage anxiety about the future by creating beliefs that make us comfortable. In business we call it "planning," an educated guess about how things will be in the future. Clearly, planning is valuable. It gets everyone moving in the same direction. But, failing to recognize that hoped-for outcomes can be illusions about the future can cause us to miss seeing when things are not working and when we must re-route to get what we need. Being able to accept whatever happens in the future with the confidence that we can handle it in a constructive manner lets us have the full use of our abilities.

Complaining

Complaining is often a regular part of our business day, particularly at lunch with co-workers. Once someone starts, it becomes addictive—complaints start jumping out of the woodwork. Complaints can be clues to hidden agendas, including conscious attempts at emotional manipulation. And, for listeners who love to hear people complaining about others, it can be a clue to their unresolved personal emotional roadblocks.

When listening to a complaint, keep in mind the complaint may not be putting the real issue on the table. When you take someone's words at face value, you can be lead astray. The complainer may simply be out of touch with what is bothering him or unable or unwilling to tell you. The same is true with your own complaints. If you take them at face value, you can block your progress. So when complaints surface, dig deeper to see if there are hidden issues. If you don't see any, use the complaint as a clue to a possible roadblock you may need to work around. Remember the situation with Anthony? I could have worked around that roadblock if I had acknowledged my complaining about Anthony for what it really was—avoiding a reality about Anthony I didn't want to see.

BREAKTHROUGH INSIGHT: If you find yourself chronically complaining about other people, consider the possibility that you are not happy with yourself. When you are able to stop complaining about others, there is little doubt that you are feeling better about yourself. Think about it.

Your reaction to a complaint can be a valuable clue to an underlying roadblock. For example, how do you feel when someone complains to you about, say, your company? The next time it happens, write your immediate thoughts in your Development Diary. How you feel or react can signal something within you getting in your way, and can be a clue to how you feel about yourself.

Pay attention to any nuances in how you react to complaints. For example, you may feel differently about a complaint depending on who is doing the complaining. If it's a friend, you may react one way. If it's a stranger, you may react quite differently. And the difference may be dictated by how you want to appear to the complainer. So, when you are on the receiving end of a complaint, take note of how you react. If you find over time that you react differently to similar complaints depending on who the complainer is, dig deep to identify why the same complaint makes you feel differently. A cocktail party complainer, for example, may ruffle the image you want to portray about your prowess in business or your level of intelligence. If you're not feeling good about yourself at the time of the complaint, you may be more likely to be offended or defensive. If on the other hand you're relaxed and confident, you're less likely to take the complaint personally, and you'll see the complainer as a person with problems of his own.

Properly handled, complaints provide strategic opportunities to move forward—they're clues that can affect your success strategy. A successful sales person, for example, might use complaints to solidify customer relationships. His customer may, in effect, be saying "I'm unhappy, please do something about it." When a customer is unhappy and says nothing, it's likely he will take his business elsewhere. If the salesperson were to become defensive, rather than strategic, he could lose the opportunity to continue a dialogue and establish a good working relationship. Skillful sales people don't take complaints personally, or even if they do, they keep their emotions in check.

BREAKTHROUGH INSIGHT: People, particularly those with low self-esteem, often take any apparent complaint personally and act out inappropriately. Doing this is clearly self-destructive.

Anxiety

Anxiety is a great clue to possible hidden issues holding you or others back. Many things, real or imagined, make us anxious. When these things are imagined, more likely than not we inadvertently manage our anxieties in a way that is ultimately self-destructive. A classic example of this is people always being afraid of being fired. They're quick to misread what is said or happening as a threat to their jobs, and, all too often, they say or do something that actually puts them at risk.

Anxious people are always in high gear blocking or rationalizing away their upset. Some head for the local bar, others grab a tranquilizer, some lose their temper at the drop of a hat, some keep themselves frantically busy and some masterfully create comforting illusions. Only the symptoms, not the cause, are relieved. There's nothing wrong with getting rid of symptoms as long as we acknowledge the possibility that we are not eliminating underlying emotional conflicts that could block progress.

Keep in mind: When we act to mask anxiety, we risk developing unconscious behavior patterns that cloud access to our full capabilities. For example, people anxious about flying often avoid jobs requiring extensive air travel, and miss solid career opportunities.

BREAKTHROUGH INSIGHT: Eliminating painful situations makes perfect sense. If your hand hurt when you put it in a fire, you wouldn't put it in a fire. Nor would you leave it there until you figured out why it hurt! With anxiety, the story can be different. If you quickly rid yourself of the symptom, rather than live with it and explore the fact that it may be hampering your progress, you miss an opportunity to eliminate or end-run an emotional roadblock.

Facing our personal limitations, real or imagined, can make us anxious. But, when we avoid doing this to stay anxiety free, we limit our capabilities and block progress.

We have what we have. And vice versa. Accepting our limitations, even if not well-founded, does not change our innate abilities in business. But accepting the way we are, or the way we think we are, frees us to move on. For example, if you feel you are not THE absolute smartest person in your company, so what? First of all, there is no way to know this. And second, intelligence can sometimes hinder more than help. It's great for school, but not necessarily for business. If you feel you must be THE smartest person around, you may have been raised by a disapproving parent with a destructive emotional agenda. As a child, you weren't in a position to figure that out. But as an adult you are. So, if you are preoccupied with not feeling smart enough, this may be a clue to a destructive roadblock you've been carrying around far too long. This illusion can clearly block your progress.

BREAKTHROUGH INSIGHT: People are often preoccupied with intelligence—their own and that of others. This is something often so ingrained during school years that they never gain the right perspective on its value. For example, when we're told someone is smart, we often defer to their demands. But in doing so, we put ourselves at risk by not questioning their judgment. Never forget, intelligence does not equate to common sense, good business judgment, experience or moral values. And it clearly does not override destructive emotional issues. If you're intimidated by so-called brilliance, you will limit your capabilities, opportunities and the full use of your talent.

So, when you're anxious in a business situation, don't let all the anxiety go to waste! Make written notes in your Diary of what you're experiencing. This will help you firmly acknowledge clues to underlying progress blocks. When the situation has played itself out, revisit what you've written to see whether the reasons for your anxieties were validly based. If you do this each time you're anxious in business, you'll eventually see that most of your concerns are the product of an overactive imagination. Or, if there is some truth to what you were anxious about, you'll learn to accept it and work around it.

For example, let's say you're a bit insecure, not having a particularly good day, and your boss walks by you in the hallway without saying hello. How do you think you might feel? Rejected? Would you be anxious about your hopes for a promotion? If so, you're not alone. But, if you allow your anxiety to take hold, you might act in a way that puts you at risk. On the other hand, if you felt confident, you may clearly see your boss is no different than you are when under pressure. And that may have been the only reason he did not acknowledge you.

BREAKTHROUGH INSIGHT: The bottom line for success in business is believing you're able to achieve whatever you want. Hanging on to old illusions about yourself does not pay the bills, particularly when your worst fears or anxieties about yourself are totally unfounded or absolutely unreasonable.

Negative Thinking

Negative thinking is a product of, and a clue to, a massive hidden self-destructive agenda. There are absolutely no ifs, ands or buts.

What's interesting about negative thinkers is that they believe they can predict when choices will work but rarely, if ever, when choices will work. Unfortunately, most negative thinkers rarely reach their full potential, even though they often have a small measure of success in advisory roles. What they fail to see, along with the listeners who go along with them, is that their own marginal track record disqualifies them from making good business assessments.

BREAKTHROUGH INSIGHT: If the person giving you advice is not where you'd like to be, don't lose sight of the fact that his or her advice is based upon a faulty track record. And when the track record is not good, chances are the advice is not either.

So what could negative people be thinking about the value of the advice they're offering? More likely than not, nothing. They're simply and frantically trying to stay within their emotional comfort zone. In the face of business uncertainty, negative thinking eliminates uncomfortable risks. For them, avoiding uncertainty trumps success. When others go ahead and something goes wrong, they can look brilliant. The "If you had only listened to me" statement works every time! For negative people it's better to fail by not trying than to risk failing.

BREAKTHROUGH INSIGHT: If you get upset when you hear a negative comment, use that as a clue to the possibility of negativity within yourself. Very often, negative people make us uncomfortable because their negativity makes us aware of our own.

Negative people are terrified of knowing they're negative. They go to great lengths to let everyone, including themselves, believe they're practical or realistic thinkers. Ever met anyone who wanted something and, in the very next breath, said he probably wouldn't get it? Did he try to cover his negativity by telling you he was just being realistic? The next time someone is negative about something you say, point out they seem quite negative. Use the word "negative" and then stand back and listen to the cover-up response.

BREAKTHROUGH INSIGHT: In identifying whether you think negatively, be careful not to let your own labeling of what you are doing mislead you. You may, for example, feel that you're just weighing the pros and cons of a situation, rather than being negative. Be honest with yourself. Negative people are masters at covering up recognizing their negativity. Don't be one of them!

Negative thinkers often avoid confronting their negativity by cleverly not taking responsibility for their negative decisions. Did you ever run into a man who always consults his wife about exciting new business opportunities that might involve some risk? He gets angry if she tells him not to get involved. And he doesn't. Typically, whenever he talks to his wife about business ventures, he always gets the same negative response, yet he always consults her. He is influenced, and therefore limited, by her comments. At least, he thinks, he's held back by her comments, rather than his fears. Invariably, if you were to talk to him about what he said to his wife, you might discover he actually steered his wife into a negative response by not fully presenting the positive side. And, by doing so, he created a way out he could live with. Instead of hiding his negative inclination behind a "being realistic" position, he hid it behind an "it was all her fault that I missed a real opportunity" statement.

BREAKTHROUGH INSIGHT: Is there someone in your life who discourages you from acting by always throwing cold water on your ideas? If so, how do you respond to the criticism? Do you challenge it, get mad, or quietly walk away discouraged? More importantly, do you continually go back to that person for advice? If it's the latter, this is a clue that the real roadblock is within you.

YOUR AWARENESS DEVELOPMENT EXERCISE

The next time you're involved with a negative person, watch your reaction closely. Write down all thoughts in your Development Diary. Getting advice from someone who is negative, or "realistic," and letting that advice influence you may be an unconscious way you express your own negativity.

Once you've done that take a moment and write in your Development Diary how you would feel if you found out you are generally negative. List all the thoughts that go through your mind regardless of whether you think they are related to thinking negatively. Think about:

- Whether or not you would be embarrassed to have someone believe you are a negative person.
- What being a negative person means to you?
- How do you feel about being around someone who thinks negatively?
- What you would do if you hired a person who turned out to be negative.
- Whether you believe that a negative thinker actually blocks his progress in business.

The answers may give you some clues into your unconscious agendas in business.

BREAKTHROUGH INSIGHT: Realizing you're negative may be hard to accept, but never miss the chance to explore the possibility and eliminate it. If you discover that you are negative in business situations, be thankful you found out. Ignoring it won't change it. Acknowledging it provides the opportunity to deal with it constructively.

Embarrassment

Feeling embarrassed can be a clue to an underlying progress block. If you, for example, live in fear of making embarrassing mistakes or doing or saying something silly, that preoccupation creates stress, which in turn interferes with your ability to function at your best. Under stress your measurable IQ drops and you're less likely to think clearly. Worse yet, a destructive part of you may unconsciously cause mistakes as a way of sabotaging your progress.

The fact is that we all make mistakes or do or say silly things from time to time—that's simply a fact of life. If you have no underlying roadblocks, you may be momentarily embarrassed, but you will be able to put the incident into proper perspective and move forward. But, if you can't, use that as a clue to a self-destructive possibility within yourself.

So, when you're embarrassed, see if you can identify why. You may find it was not what someone did or said, but, rather, that he triggered an old feeling about yourself that no longer should have a valid place in your life. As with other clues to hidden roadblocks within yourself, use embarrassment as a way to look at something within yourself that you either need to eliminate or learn to work around.

The same is true when someone you're dealing with is embarrassed. Be alert to how he may damage your progress. Embarrassed people sometimes, to save face, get rigidly locked into positions that can block progress, both for you and for them.

YOUR AWARENESS DEVELOPMENT SITUATION

Suppose you just completed a lengthy report for your boss. You read and re-read the report to make sure it was perfect. You're now sitting in his office as he goes over it. He pauses and asks the meaning of a particular sentence. When you look at it, it's clear several words were dropped. Overtired when finalizing the report, you missed the typos. Take a moment and write in your Development Diary what you would say to him. How do you think you would feel inside?

Let's go a little further. If you have not already addressed the following issues in your Development Diary, take another moment and do so:

- If you would have been embarrassed, see if you can identify why.
- Would you tell your boss how you felt inside?
- Are you hard on yourself when you make mistakes?
- Do you think the mistake would affect your relationship with your boss?

If you think that a mistake like this would affect you in a significant way, keep track in your Diary of similar mistakes you make until you see if a pattern develops. A pattern might show how you think or what preoccupies you when you have to do something for your boss or a person in authority. On the other hand, failing to understand that mistakes are inevitable in any business process can be an insight into a hidden roadblock. It's not possible to flawlessly execute everything you do. Success comes from being realistic and effectively recovering from mistakes.

Being Critical

People constantly criticizing others are often obsessively criticizing themselves. Pay attention if you find yourself criticizing everyone, or a particular person or type of person. Criticizing others or yourself can be a clue to destructive issues within yourself, something that can block capabilities and progress.

BREAKTHROUGH INSIGHT: If you constantly criticize a particular person, think about why you continue to engage with that person—assuming you have a choice. It could be your way of insuring there is always someone close at hand to make you feel better about yourself. Or it may your way of unknowingly holding yourself back.

Have you ever heard of a man who fires one female secretary after another? He says he can't find one that will do the job right. Then the personnel department gives him a male secretary. And everything works smoothly. For whatever reason, he couldn't deal with women. An issue never resolved in his personal life was resolved for him in his business life. If he had known what his roadblock was, he could have hired a male secretary as a way to end-run his roadblock. With less conflict, he would have been more productive, and looked less crippled.

A point to remember: If you have an emotional roadblock, work within its restraints. It may be hard to admit that you may have destructive emotional issues for reasons we all know full well, but it is better than suffering economically.

BREAKTHROUGH INSIGHT: We all came into a world with destructive philosophies. It's a waste of time trying to change it so you feel you can function effectively. Your effort must be to learn how not to be a victim, and move yourself forward doing whatever is necessary—including realistically working with the limits in front of you.

One final point about criticism. If you're working or are involved with someone who constantly criticizes you or others, that criticism is a valuable insight into his emotional makeup, particularly if it's unfair. The person may have a low opinion of himself or be constantly judging himself. Wasting time trying to understand why can be a clue to your unwillingness to move forward and is a useless exercise. So, when you're around someone who is constantly criticizing you or others, your sole objective must be to develop a realistic strategy to eliminate or effectively manage what is happening. If your boss is unfairly critical of you, the solution may be to look for another job. If a member of your work team is constantly criticizing every new idea, eliminate the person from your team or develop another strategy so the criticism does not kill your spirit and progress.

Job Fantasies

If you find yourself constantly fantasizing about aspects of your job that you'd like change but cannot, use that as a clue that you may be blocking your progress. And if you are working with someone constantly fantasizing about similar changes to his work situation, accept the possibility that this person has roadblocks hampering his progress and maybe yours.

For example, do you ever fantasize about how much easier your job would be if a particular situation or person was different? If you have a difficult boss, do you daydream about his quitting or being fired? Any thoughts about what would make you happier—a nicer office or working on the executive's floor?

AN AWARENESS DEVELOPMENT EXERCISE

Take a moment and make note in your Development Diary of any changes that would make you happier in your job or business, particularly ones that you have daydreamed about. Are there any that you could have made but didn't? If so, write down why you didn't. If you feel stuck with the way things are, how does that make you feel? Do you say it is because of factors you can't control?

Now, think about this if you're in a difficult work environment that seems to be blocking your progress: Have you ever considered the possibility that you unconsciously put yourself in a work environment in which you feel helpless? And the trap may be of your own making? So, if you're in a spot you do not like now that you're thinking about it, don't concern yourself. Spending hours analyzing the whys of your actions can distract you from seeing the real issues and the solutions. Your objective is just to see that you are in the spot.

Frustration and Giving Up

Even with the best planning and resources, things go wrong. We fail. And we become frustrated. Some push ahead, but many give up. Those that quit, lose. So, if you're frustrated and want to give up, dig deep. Quitting because you're frustrated is a clue to a possible self-destructive tendency, an inner roadblock. Worse yet, if you have a tendency to give up simply because it's taking too long to achieve your goals, you have a serious progress roadblock in play.

BREAKTHROUGH INSIGHT: It stands to reason that those who give up trying as soon as they become frustrated won't get what they want. So, if you want to give up as soon as you're frustrated, be honest about what you're feeling so you don't sabotage yourself.

Frustration can be self-manufactured—a setup excuse to give up. If you've ever set a personal goal to meet by a certain time and, frustrated, felt like a failure because the deadline passed, you're a victim of a personal self-destructive agenda that needs addressing. Setting a time goal is fine, but you must consider fairly why the deadline was missed. If it was because of uncontrollable factors, such as changes in the economy or market demand or your own unrealistic view, and you still feel like you failed, chances are good you have a serious progress roadblock. And if you're working with someone else who is constantly frustrated about missing goals, that person may have a roadblock that could be interfering with job progress.

BREAKTHROUGH INSIGHT: People who set unrealistic goal time frames unconsciously set themselves up for frustration and failure.

A business acquaintance of mine was a pro at the frustration game. Almost every time we had dinner, he would say he was out to make a million dollars. Over the years he searched for that one deal that he thought would do the job for him. As soon as he got involved in a project, within a matter of days he would become frustrated if he thought the project would not produce a million dollars virtually overnight. He either sabotaged the project by being negative or completely abandoned it and began looking around for another million dollar baby. Each time we got together, he was either excited over a new project, depressed because he could not find one, or frustrated because it was not happening at the speed he wanted. He spent years looking for the fast hit instead of sticking with a project that could eventually get him what he wanted. He liked to talk about the fast buck deal. It did create an aura about him. He wanted everyone to know he was a wheeler-dealer, the hot shot of his business and social circles. The clue to his underlying emotional roadblock was the chronic frustration that pushed him to quit. He was unsure of himself and did not want anyone to see him fail on a project. He still experiences frustration year after year, as he passes from one deal to another.

So, when frustration surfaces, and you or others want to give up, carefully, honestly and realistically assess why. As I've said, quitting when you are frustrated is a great clue to a possible inner roadblock.

Depression

Depression can signal the existence of many psychological issues far too complex to address here. Some are serious and some are not. It may simply result from being tired or momentarily disappointed. But it may also surface when something has touched a personal issue too painful to acknowledge. Whatever the cause, it's something that should not be ignored. And if it's prolonged, professional help is recommended, particularly if it's chronic. In any event, it can be a clue to an underlying emotional roadblock stifling progress, the cause of which must be addressed. For example, if you become more than momentarily depressed because you didn't get an expected raise or promotion, it may signal an underlying feeling of low self-esteem. Low self-esteem clearly will block progress.

So, use depression as a possible clue to uncover a roadblock. If it's not chronic and prolonged and you can sit with it, rather than frantically trying to distract yourself, chances are that its cause will surface. In many cases, you'll find the cause was based on unrealistic and ingrained beliefs. And, if so, you have the opportunity to eliminate what no longer has a valid place in your life.

BREAKTHROUGH INSIGHT: Depression is sometimes anger turned inward--anger that we can't express directly.

A great example of how unrealistic beliefs can cause depression is the woman who continually looks for Mr. Right. The search is invariably unsuccessful. Each time a relationship falls apart, she becomes depressed. She never sees her role in the breakup and always blames the man. Her worst fears of always being alone flood her thoughts. "Why is it so difficult to meet the right person?" she asks herself. What she never realizes is, even after years of looking, odds are good she may be the problem. She never uses her depression as a clue to see if she could have an underlying self-destructive issue. Maybe for good reasons. Facing the truth could force personal issues to surface that are far more painful than being alone. But by facing any underlying issues, she might have been able to free herself and find happiness. The same can be true for men in a similar situation.

YOUR AWARENESS DEVELOPMENT EXERCISE

When you're depressed, write down your random thoughts in your Development Diary. Don't think. Don't analyze. Just write and see what you discover. If you have difficulty, try a visualization or relaxation exercise like one in Chapter 12. Then try writing your thoughts down.

When you're relaxed, it's easier to look inward to find real underlying issues. You might find that the depression is gone once you're relaxed. When that happens, it's likely that the cause was something minor, such as being overtired.

The point is that when you experience a possible clue to an underlying roadblocking inclination, depression or anything else, take a close look at it. See if you can determine the cause or any patterns. Always write your thoughts down in your Development Diary.

Worry

People worry when they fear an outcome will be bad from their point of view. Worry is natural, but not when it's chronic. The act of worrying fills your mind with clutter that blocks your thinking process and your ability to use your talents to the fullest. And it is a clue to a progress roadblock lurking beneath the surface of your conscious mind.

If you don't see how worry clutters your or anyone else's mind, pay attention the next time you talk to someone worried about a problem. See if he's really listening to you. Is he resisting constructive suggestions or negative about them? Look at his eyes. Are they darting back and forth? Do they look glazed over? If so, rest assured that his mind is so filled with thought static that he can't process what you're saying.

YOUR AWARENESS DEVELOPMENT EXERCISE

If you find yourself worrying, see if there is something that you can learn about yourself. Be alert to worry as a clue to a possible emotional roadblock. Keep track, in your Development Diary, of each worry to see if a pattern develops so you can look back and see how valid your worry was.

For example:

- Did you survive what you felt was the worst outcome if it came to pass?
- Do your worst fears come to pass often?
- Do you worry about issues that cannot be controlled?
- Did you try to do something realistic to eliminate your worry?

In the future, turn a worry situation into one that will provide new opportunities. People who refuse to worry excessively will tell you that everything always works out for the best, even if they did not think it would at the time. The man who always worried about being fired and who was fired and then went on to build an empire is a familiar story. He would tell you that being fired was the best thing that ever happened to him. Interestingly, he probably stuck with his job for all the wrong reasons. And he may have unconsciously set himself up to be fired to create an opportunity that he was unable to create consciously.

BREAKTHROUGH INSIGHT: Worry is based upon what you think will happen. And inevitably worry is an outgrowth of a profound negative inclination. Spend some time with your worries and see what you can learn about yourself that may be holding you back!

Difficulty in Listening

People who have difficulty paying attention limit their business potential. When someone is unable to listen, assuming it's not a legitimate learning disability, it's often because they're struggling to keep feelings about themselves from surfacing, such as being afraid of looking stupid or feeling as though they won't be able to perform. And their struggle may go off the charts when they're talking to their boss or someone who they think is smarter or better in some way

Problem listeners respond in a variety of ways to cover up. Some are defensive.

Others avoid dialogues that would make it evident they can't listen by, for example, controlling the conversation. Not hearing other points of view is preferable to feeling lost or looking stupid. Too consumed with personal fears or issues, rarely do they realize their inability to follow the conversation is caused by an emotional block, not a lack of intelligence.

Some problem listeners learn to cope by taking notes. It may look silly at times, but it's better than looking or being incompetent. Those who haven't learned to cope often become destructive by being very aggressive. For them, it's better to look smart than to succeed, a dangerous emotional state to be in. If you are relying in business on someone whom you suspect may be caught in this trap, you need to be extremely careful for obvious reasons.

So, when you spot an inability to pay attention, either in yourself or someone else, use it as a clue to an underlying progress roadblock that needs to be addressed. And if it's chronic in you, consider getting professional help. It can be a major success roadblock.

Avoiding Pressure

People who constantly try to avoid "pressure" are running away from underlying conflicts. The pressure they're avoiding is often internal pressure of their own making, and not from a legitimate outside source. Avoiding pressure is an underlying roadblock clue.

If this might describe you, the key is to honestly determine whether you're experiencing inner or outer pressure. A filing clerk can feel as much pressure as a CEO of a major corporation, obviously for different reasons. But whatever the reason, feeling under pressure will adversely limit a person's ability to effectively process information and perform well. As I've stated earlier, it's been shown that the measurable IQ of people under stress drops.

YOUR AWARENESS DEVELOPMENT EXERCISE

If during a day you feel under pressure, write your thoughts in your Development Diary. In the evening, try to identify all the causes and the thoughts that passed through your mind. For example:
- Is the pressure external or internal?
- Describe how you felt at the time you experienced the pressure.
  - Were you afraid you were going to be fired or lose your business?
  - Were there other concerns, such as fearing someone would laugh at you?

- Did the pressure come from what you thought would happen, or was it something that actually happened?
- List everything you can remember in the past when you felt similar pressure and write down what the outcome was.
  - Did you survive it?
  - Do you think you had a hand in anything bad happening?

Treat an attempt to avoid pressure the same way you treat other clues to potential underlying emotional problems. Work with it—see what turns up. Explore your inner thoughts. If it's someone you're working with, develop a strategy to ensure that your progress is not hampered.

Frantic Activity or Busy Work

When people engage in mindless frantic activities or busy work, they're running from inner issues that can block progress. The activity distracts them from uncomfortable feelings and thoughts—in effect, it blocks them out of their mind, much like creating a distraction by turning the volume up high on a radio.

Frantic activity or busy work is a clue to inner emotional issues that will limit a person's ability to reach his potential—and, for that matter, even having real peace or happiness in his life. As with any other type of clue, when you feel the need to run constantly, take a moment and jot your thoughts down in your Diary. Look for causes and patterns that you need to eliminate or end-run inner roadblocks, so your progress is not blocked simply to avoid moments of discomfort.

Excessive Drinking or Drugs

Excessive drinking or drugs....enough said. A top clue to an inner progress roadblock for you or someone you're working with! Some people rationalize their drinking or drug use as manageable or desirable. Those who do are MASSIVELY self-destructive.

If this describes you, getting professional help is the only course of action. If it's someone you're working with and he cannot, for whatever reasons, get professional help, it's time to change the relationship. It cannot be managed. And any belief that you can manage it is a clue to a possible self-destructive tendency within yourself.

And the Clues Go On

As stated at the start of the clues discussion, I am not suggesting that what I've described are all the possible clues to underlying progress roadblocks. They're only a sampling of ones that you should be on the lookout for—both in yourself and in others.

As you open up to the possibility of clues and how your inner blocking agenda may be working you over, you will identify others. For example, things such as an inability to control anger, moments of hysteria, an obsession with a particular objective, compulsive behavior, a need to control others, judging the future based on past experience only and needing to dress a certain way may all be clues to an emotional agenda that you should pay careful attention to—to ensure nothing is getting in your way

Don't concern yourself with proving beyond a doubt whether what appears to be a clue is in fact one. Doing so in and of itself may be a clue to a roadblock within you. If you suspect that you've spotted a clue, trust that you have and work with it. Very simply, use anything that you may suspect to be a clue to prompt you to dig deeper for progress roadblocks. And be easy on yourself.

Do not forget: Anything that may be a clue to an underlying roadblock in yourself is not something you should feel guilty or bad about. Underlying roadblocks that you have not insisted on holding onto are ones that you came to honestly and without your conscious participation. If you're very concerned about any, again, get professional input. And, for some, just treat them as a human eccentricity, as long as they don't damage your ability to achieve peace and happiness in both your personal and business life. For these, accept them with a bit of humor--and eventually you'll see they have little, if any, influence on your progress.

Finally, once you've identified what you think may be a clue to an underlying, and destructive, emotional agenda, your objective is to develop a strategy to eliminate or end-run it, something I'll show you how to do as you read on.

Summary

We are all hampered, to a greater or lesser extent, by hidden and unconscious emotional roadblocks to our progress, both in our personal and our business life. The key to eliminating or end-running those that get in our way is to look for clues to emotional undercurrents that impede your progress. When you think you've found a clue, trust that you have—even if later you discover you've misread what you thought was a clue. The more you are able to identify clues and the less afraid you are to be honest about what is happening, the faster you will progress.

Chapter 7

INTEGRATING THE BASICS

Got the Clues, Now What?

As I've discussed, if you suspect hidden agendas are sabotaging your business efforts, look for clues. A clue won't necessarily tell what's occurring, or for that matter that something is in fact occurring, but it will alert you to look for other indications that could confirm a hidden emotional agenda.

In the beginning, it takes effort to overcome tendencies you may have to rationalize away what may be occurring. Over time, however, it will be easier as you put into perspective all misleading rationalizations, illusions, agendas, feelings, beliefs and needs. The key to all of this is accepting yourself and others as you and they are, without recrimination or judgment. When you can, rest assured that you will have arrived at a point of unique business clarity, which will pay untold dividends for you.

As you become comfortable accepting reality, you'll see individual behavior patterns you never noticed before, and you'll understand ones that never made any sense to you. It will dawn on you that all of these are giant clues staring you smack in the face to possible roadblocking agendas. Then, you'll gain the insights needed to overcome obstacles, both in yourself and in others.

Your ultimate objective in spotting clues is to use them to develop strategies to progress in a way best for you, and to do this without harming those well-meaning people around you unknowingly getting in your way—and, of course, those not-so-well-meaning folks intentionally trying to block your progress. Keep in mind, there is no one-size-fits-all answer for any given situation––there are too many subtle variables. Developing effective strategies to eliminate or end-run progress blocks will often be a trial and error process. But your new clarity will allow you to find approaches that will move you forward.

BREAKTHROUGH INSIGHT: The challenge we face in moving past hidden destructive agendas, in ourselves and in others, is overcoming our subconscious inner monster whose sole purpose is keep us in our comfort zone, something that interferes with our clear perception of what is occurring. Very simply, you have to learn to emotionally balance what you see in others and in yourself against your reactions to what you are seeing.

Surrounded by Complexity

Now let's begin the process of integrating what you've learned. The human condition is complex. Feelings run our show—and the show of others. Good ones and bad ones. Ones we're aware of and ones so buried beneath mountains of convoluted beliefs and rationalizations we miss them. Identifying when destructive ones we don't see in ourselves or others are in play is our goal.

As you now know, the first place to start to eliminate progress blocks is with yourself—the only person you really have any control over. One excellent way to find roadblock issues within yourself is to look at the people you bring into, or keep in, your life. Their emotional characteristics will inevitably be a clue to where you are emotionally. If, for example, you bring negative people into your life or business environment, this is a solid clue that, unconsciously, you have chosen to hold yourself back without accepting the responsibility for doing it.

Once you determine where you are emotionally, you will systematically and intuitively be able to develop ways to move yourself forward using techniques and awarenesses in this book. To move yourself forward, however, never forget that your progress depends on being brutally honest about any clues that surface and about the real basis for your rationalizations and reactions to the people around you.

Time to Meet Some Fun Business Personalities

Let's kick-start your awareness by working with some fictional, composite personalities. You'll undoubtedly see traits, mannerisms and personality styles that will, in bits and pieces, ring bells about people whom you know and work with. These are all manifestations of underlying emotional issues, needs and agendas. Any one trait or mannerism signals underlying issues which may be harmless, but finding any in someone you're working with should alert you to possible issues that might slow you down. However, be kind; we're all a package of complex emotional eccentricities—the people who become crippled are those whose non-productive feelings override the productive feelings for reasons only the most qualified mental health professionals can sort through.

I'm going to begin your process of learning how to identify and deal with people who are awash with clues and who inevitably block progress by being playful and a bit silly. It's the best way to look at issues that might be uncomfortable. And if you sense discomfort within yourself, that may be a clue to dig deeper for possible progress blocks. So, here we go!

Say hello to three solid business citizens: Edison Energy, III, Betty B. Buster and Nedbert Neatly. These pillars of the business community are fictional personality composites of characteristics found in real people. See if you can link any characteristics of Edison, Betty or Nedbert with any of your problem business associates. If you can, you may start to realize how he or she could possibly be getting in your way. These fictional personality types exhibit a multitude of giant clues, some of which undoubtedly stare you in the face each business day.

The profiles of Edison, Betty and Nedbert are designed to begin helping you integrate all parts of various emotional puzzle pieces. Each mannerism or personality trait that Edison, Betty and Nedbert have can be a clue to an underlying emotional issue that may be trouble, particularly if handled improperly.

Finally, keep in mind these folks are purely fictional, but their profiles have been designed and discussed to show you how various possible underlying emotional issues important to look for and understand can surface. Some may provoke feelings within you. If one trait is particularly offensive or unsettling to you, that is your clue to something within you that needs to be addressed so you don't set up roadblocks for yourself. And remember, not accepting or reacting inappropriately to any particular personality issue can result in a progress block, or a business distraction.

Edison Energy, III

Edison Energy, III is a sly fellow. He is usually bright, personable on the surface and totally preoccupied with his career. Edison always gets in the office before everyone else. This, of course, is so he can get some work done "before the phone starts ringing." Edison is quite creative, but he avoids acknowledging it fully, especially to others who may extrapolate too far with what may be considered a feminine trait. After all, heaven knows Edison is ALL man!

Edison has been raised by an emotionally destructive parent, which prevented him from achieving a rational level of self-confidence. What's never really apparent to those around him is that he is very sensitive, very jealous of others and competitive to a fault. He likes to believe, for example, that his house is more expensive than any other person in his social or business circle. He compensates for his lack of confidence by name dropping, particularly when socializing with his superiors. He believes that if his circle of friends includes well-known people, others will make the assumption that he must be worth knowing. One implication, of course, is that with all his connections he may put any nifty deal together for you. So, hint, hint, don't forget to include him in any venture!

His marital situation is the pits, but not necessarily on the surface. Just to be on the safe side, he married the first girl that kissed him on a date. At least he thought it was a kiss. After that, it was always taken for granted by his would-be wife that they would be married. So Edison complied. The decision was made for him.

Edison's wife has what many would consider masculine traits. She's hard-driving, domineering, emotionally cold and very independent. As a result, his home is impeccable and his home life is picture perfect, but Edison is silently unhappy about it. He secretly fantasizes about having an affair with the pretty woman down the street. However, he does little more than think about his fantasy because he is absolutely petrified of getting caught by his wife, a parental figure who would level him in no uncertain terms.

How does Edison live with himself? He blocks feeling the depth of his unhappiness by diving into his work. Unfortunately, his entire self-worth depends on his job. He feels good or bad about himself during his business day depending on whether or not he got some form of recognition within the last few minutes. Edison does not like to take vacations unless they are something he can boast about to his friends and co-workers, stays at a distance from his children lest he get in touch with his attachment feelings and does not seek counseling help until he falls so hard he can't get up. He usually keeps his career advancement under control, so to speak, by unconsciously sabotaging himself. His career struggle is his way of distracting himself from dealing with upsetting personal issues.

Ms. Betty B. Buster

Ms. Betty B. Buster is another classic. She's right up there with Edison Energy. Betty is bullet proof, aggressive, decisive, organized and all business. And has the sense of humor of a garden rock. She's rarely married, having decided "to take the career route." Of course, it's never emotionally apparent to Betty B that one can have both, but, in her mind, the choice makes perfect sense. Fortunately for Betty B in today's society, the career excuse is yet another accepted business rationale for an inability to relate well to men. It keeps people from wondering—at least too much.

Betty B is easy to recognize by her hairstyle and the crisp, gray, pin-striped suits she wears. Betty B's shoes are as efficient as her hair style and suits. The heels are about three-quarters of an inch long and two inches wide. Betty B has a commanding walk, typically exploding down with her all weight on the backside of her heels each time she takes a step.

Betty B has some interesting male/female relationship characteristics. Sorry, Edison, beaten again! She's actually more frightened about having to deal with the opposite sex than is Edison. Betty B is basically angry at men. A good clue to this is her constant comment that men are her best friends. No one man in particular, of course. The anonymous male figure creeps into all her conversations. Hopefully for the anonymous male, he remains anonymous. Rarely is a male a match for Betty B. She is a business ninja.

Her anger at men comes out in many ways. She can, for example, "nail a male" under the guise of suggesting a much better way to do something. Betty B is dedicated to proving there is a genetic connection between lack of competence and being a male. She has never learned to be a business person; she is a business WOMAN. Betty B often uses the courtesies afforded a woman to manipulate the male in a business setting. She wishes she were a male. "Things in business would be much easier," Betty B secretly thinks—and sometimes in a moment of frustration, admits openly.

Betty B has a male friend from time to time who is a modern version of a reincarnated teddy bear. Teddy has an abundance of society-described feminine traits. Are you getting the picture about Betty B and Teddy? Invariably, Betty B begins to have some feelings for Teddy. And, then, she quickly puts some emotional light years between Teddy and herself. Ultimately, she levels her verbal cannon at this poor soul and "the ungrateful so and so" is history. Sorry, Teddy, see you next time around.

Betty B has certainly done her small part to truly advance the cause for women in business. Her tough-mindedness and clear talent have assisted in breaking the grip that a male chauvinist cultural attitude has had on women in the business environment. She has no doubt helped the cause of women in business; unfortunately she did not help herself on the personal front. Often so consumed by anger at being limited, she becomes preoccupied with thinking how men always get in a woman's way in business—and, at times, sabotages her progress in business by verbally and succinctly cutting the legs off any male she's not happy with. For Betty B, however, the male issue is only an excuse for her not to take responsibility for dealing with her real inner fears and anxieties, something she's so terrified of touching that she orchestrates a full contingent of outside distractions to keep from hitting what is bothering her most, bad feelings about herself. Betty B is an absolute master at repression.

Mr. Nedbert Neatly

Mr. Nedbert Neatly is easy to recognize, not by his personality or his brains, but by his dress. Actually, I should say by his attire. Dress is a sensitive issue for Nedbert. Ned, as he likes to be called, is somewhat unimaginative but very smart and picture-perfect in his business suit.

Ned works for a large corporation and managed to secure a position of power in the business world by befriending a senior executive. Ned's hope is that by being the "big man's" valet he will be loved, fed and supplied with enough allowance to pursue his social activities. He doesn't quite want to make it to the top because he would lose his father figure and have to make decisions on his own. His inner self systematically and unconsciously monitors his progress so it can act quickly in the event his career progress is too good from his frame of reference. Once in a while Ned has a few "nips" in the evening and arrives in the office the following morning smelling of mouthwash. Ned is glib and always accommodating to his superiors. He, as you might suspect, is no match for the office ninja, Betty B. Buster. On the other hand, Ned can easily manage Edison. They can work together like two peas in a pod.

Let's take a closer look at Nedbert's wardrobe. He almost always wears dark business casual, including conservative button-down shirts, and, if he wears a tie, he wears a wildly colorful one. The colors of his ties are his connection with his inner need to break free of all restrictions society has imposed on him, something, however, he's rarely able to do. When he wears a suit, he always has a handkerchief in his suit coat pocket, rarely takes his suit coat off during the business day, and rarely unbuttons it while sitting at his desk. One of the most notable features is his shoes. They're always light, European-style thin leather shoes with tassels and are highly polished. Ned used to wear heavy shoes, the type of shoes Edison Energy wears, but they didn't afford Nedbert with the mobility he needs in evening social settings. He needs shoes he can "operate" with.

If you haven't guessed it already, Nedbert is divorced, a ladies' man and the product of another unfortunate childhood. He spends a good part of his business day chatting on the telephone with his lady friends, each of whom he manages to convince is the only important one in his life. Ned, like Betty B, is afraid of the opposite sex. The problem Ned sometimes has is that he might not always be absolutely certain which gender is the opposite sex. In reality, Ned secretly desires to have the cultural advantages of the female in our society, someone who traditionally is pursued and supported by the opposite sex. Although Ned does not "like" women, he desperately needs warmth from them. He searches endlessly for that love he never got but always wanted from his mother.

Ned thinks he wants to make it big in business. He doesn't realize his underlying motivation is really to establish a pseudo-parent relationship with his boss so that he can live out his business life in an emotionally secure environment. This is Ned's unconscious reason for keeping a governor on his career. Ned, unfortunately, has a love-hate relationship with his boss-parent figure. If the boss ignores him, Ned goes into overdrive. He then does something that gets the boss's attention, like coming up with a good business suggestion to eliminate corporate waste. Ned, because of his need for parental-type attention, limits himself. A good soul, Ned is nevertheless a confused and self-destructive business person.

In the case of Edison, Betty B and Nedbert, real success would unmask their individual personal conflicts. Their approach to business prevents them from having to deal full force with their underlying emotional anxieties. If you're involved with people who may have similar characteristics, be alert. People with deep inner conflicts, surfacing as traits, mannerisms or personal styles, can unfairly or destructively interfere with your progress.

Getting Real With Some Everyday Stereotype Personalities

Now let's take another step and look at a few discrete personality types we all encounter to see how you might develop strategies to prevent them from slowing you down. Remember, if you see them coming, you have a chance to decide what strategy you need to work with them effectively, if at all. And if you see them as they really are, and elect to work with any of them without a strategy, be assured that no matter how skillful you think you are, they will slow your progress or destroy your career. However, if you don't feel you need a strategy with any problem personalities, use that as a clue to something within you that may need to be end-run. Again these personalities are meant only to get your awareness wheels turning.

BREAKTHROUGH INSIGHT: A real advantage in recognizing emotional roadblock tendencies in others is that you'll be less apt to let any such tendency within yourself lead you astray.

The personality descriptions following are again fictional, but I've zeroed in on specific traits that are more readily identifiable in the business environment. By understanding there are emotional issues behind these, as with other, personality traits, styles and mannerisms, you will begin to look beyond the surface of what you see and accept them as clues to potential progress roadblocks for you if you suspect someone is getting in your way. The key to progress in these cases is to focus less on the personality and more on what may be driving it.

BREAKTHROUGH INSIGHT: Handling or avoiding problem people can be approached in the same manner as learning to drive. You don't have to know the intricacies of how a car engine operates to become a good driver.

One more important point to keep in mind: Although there's no doubt you will encounter ruthless or sociopathic people or downright criminals in the business environment, most problem people are not bad or evil. They're simply unconsciously controlled by defensive, survival and anxiety-based needs that end up blocking opportunities for others as well as themselves! So, in your dealings with people who are creating friction in your business efforts, stay judgment neutral. Simply assess how you're being blocked and develop a strategy for getting your objectives met. Too often we see irrational or non-businesslike behavior and spend hours, days and even years mulling over why that person is doing what he is doing—and doing that is an excuse for not taking action that will benefit you.

Mr. Big Time

Mr. Big Time, a smooth-talking, bombastic individual with a massive ego, is a classic business stereotype. He's an emotionally complex individual with many hidden personal needs and agendas that can create massive business headaches for you.

Mr. Big Time is a master at office politics, knowing instinctively how to seemingly befriend people and move them all over the chessboard to suit his needs. He addresses everyone by their first name, asks about their family and always has a ready smile. When dealing with him, never forget that his business goals directly reflect his inner needs first, and the needs of others and the business he is involved with, at best, a distant second (assuming he even cares or can process the needs of anyone other than himself.)

The Mr. Big Times have a real advantage. And they know it. When we're following the rules of fair play, they're plotting ways to use what we think the rules are against us. In fact, they know we'll stick to the fairness rules even if we're cheated. They know we'll bend over backward to rationalize away anything shady they do that we may glimpse—largely because they know most people always look for the good in others and want to believe that everyone plays fairly. But, for them, there are no rules. Business is a game. One which they know they can win by maneuvering while everyone else is looking the other way. Even if you catch them red-handed, they'll look you straight in the eye and deny what you saw. They might even convince you they didn't do what you saw them do. Or they might laugh, slap you on the back, and humbly ask for your forgiveness and promise never to do it again. And if you give them a second chance, no doubt they'll figure out a clever way to repeat it if it benefits them.

When you're involved with a Mr. Big Time, particularly if you are not self-confident or experienced in business, it can take years to catch on to what's happening, if at all. These people know how to manipulate us in ways we've never dreamed of—and certainly never learned in school. For them, a key to their disarming style is their BIG smile—something they've learned from childhood suckers most people. But their smiling, upbeat manner hides the fact that they always have their hand in your pocket grabbing any loose change or opportunities there for the taking. All the while telling you how great you are and what they're going to do for you. We often cave in to their charm simply because they're flat-out engaging and fun to be around. Secretly, they feel superior, and believe they can talk their way out of any situation in which they're caught with their hand in the business till. And often they can.

Your Strategy – Learning a Process

If you sense someone is a Mr. Big Time, but are unsure because of everything he's telling and doing for you, trust your gut. Over time, you'll find it doesn't matter if you're right as long as you're moving forward. And that is the litmus test—progress.

BREAKTHROUGH INSIGHT: Any preoccupation with whether your gut assessment about a Mr. Big Time, or any other personality you encounter, is right can be a clue to a personal roadblock interfering with your progress. The fact is there is often no way to know the inner workings of someone and spending endless hours trying to figure that out is an excuse not to get out of your comfort zone to progress. **All that should matter is ensuring your progress, even if the strategies you develop to properly handle people and yourself may not have**

been essential.

In developing a strategy for a Mr. Big Time or any other roadblock person in your life, you must be able to take a hard look at yourself. And that means honestly making an effort to see if the destructive-to-you personality in your life is actually getting in your way. Or whether you're imagining it to create a manufactured roadblock as a way to avoid taking responsibility for your own attitude or behavior. In either case, the roadblock is real, but your strategy, for obvious reason, will be different.

BREAKTHROUGH INSIGHT: You must actually experience an effective solution when your self-limiting thinking is leading you astray. Trying to intellectually understand why your progress is blocked is not enough. But changing your behavior and getting positive results, even if you don't intellectually understand why, will free you from unconscious roadblocks and lay the groundwork for their elimination. For example, patterning your behavior in a difficult situation after someone that handles the same situation successfully will free you from ingrained roadblocks you don't see. And if you can't, that is your clue that you are limiting yourself.

So if you think you have a Mr. Big Time in your life, your strategy with him should be simply one that gets you from point A to point B in a way he never sees coming. Here are some thoughts to consider:
- Never for a moment doubt that he is always operating at all times for his own betterment—as uncomfortable as it may be to accept that possibility.
- All that matters is what you proactively do to end-run any real or, yes, even imagined, roadblocks he has created.
- Don't waste time trying to figure out why he is that way he is—you'll never know. Doing so will prevent you from seeing all the clues right in front of you that will enable you to develop a strategy to move forward. So keep a close check on yourself if that's your inclination—and if you're so inclined that's a clue to a roadblock within you.
- Never forget, what you must do to take care of yourself, done properly, will not harm him; it will simply prevent him from using you.
- Trying to have an open and reasonable discussion with a Mr. Big Time is a

waste of time. It only gives him more ammunition to work you over in ways that you don't see.

- If you have a conversation with Mr. Big Time about what he is doing unfairly to you, and he says you have a good point, don't trust his response.
- Use the same tactics on him that he uses on you—he'll likely be a sucker for them. Flash the BIG smile and slap him on the back if you can get away with it. And above all, keep your feelings inside.

BREAKTHROUGH INSIGHT: People develop manipulative techniques often based upon unconscious insights into their own psychology. For example, salesmen are susceptible to the same kind of sales techniques they use on others. In formulating sales approaches, for example, they typically figure out, often unconsciously, what would work on them.

YOUR AWARENESS DEVELOPMENT SITUATION

Assume that you work for a Mr. Big Time, and that he frequently calls you around family dinner time to discuss business. If this would not trouble you, good—but take a moment to honestly think about why. And make a note of it in your Diary for future reference. The point here would be to catch yourself in needs that may not be the best for your personal well-being. Or when you might be suppressing fears and anxieties you should bring fully to the surface.

On the other hand, if it is something that could be annoying, take a moment now and think about how you would handle this situation. Don't expect a pat answer, however; there are too many variables. Before reading further, jot your ideas down in your Development Diary.

THE ANALYSIS

First, there could be many reasons why he calls at dinner time. If you spend time talking about the fact that he always calls at dinner time or trying to figure out why he does so, this preoccupation will block a solution. It could be that he's filled with so much anxiety when issues are unresolved that he is unable to hold onto his issues until the next day. He may be miserable at home, so he's using the business excuse as an escape from an uncomfortable situation. Or he may not have enough time in the day to do everything. Does it matter? No, all that matters is that he's upsetting you. You need a solution.

The challenge, then, is to figure out what to say and how to say it in a way that does not send the wrong message to Mr. Big Time, understanding that he undoubtedly has a complex personality and a big ego. He is someone who is probably self-centered and cares little about inconveniencing others. So, the first thing is to accept him as he is. This might be a personal challenge—it is for most people.

Here are some options. You could directly tell him that you would prefer to talk in the mornings in the office. What are your thoughts about how this would make you feel? Stop a moment and identify them. For example, do you think this might make him mad? Or show that you are not interested or committed enough to be one of his key people?

You might suggest that you meet for coffee before the start of each business day to discuss things he typically wants to chat about in the evening. That could serve two purposes. It shows that you're committed and may put an end to the evening calls. Or you could make a point of stopping by his office at day's end to chat. And if nothing seems to work, you might simply have to accept that talking in the evening is part of your job. If that is unacceptable, consider looking for another job rather than continue with a counterproductive distraction.

In situations like these, if you find there is no solution, or the possible solution is something you are unable to comes to terms with as part of the job, then permitting it to continue and complaining is something that you're likely using to avoid an underlying personal issue—one that could be blocking your progress—such as finding it uncomfortable to change jobs. In any event, always remember you have options. And if these options require that you move out of your zone of comfort, pursue them. Doing so will force you to grow. On the other hand, if you prefer to hunker down in your comfort zone, you will continue to suffer.

Never Forget: The real obstacle facing you in moving forward to solve a Mr. Big Time problem, or for that matter any other problem with a difficult person, is inevitably your pattern of thinking...not what is or may be actually occurring. An imagined obstacle is as dangerous as a real one. Once you think you're stuck, and you become preoccupied with what you think is happening, you are in fact stuck without a solution. The man continually complaining that his wife won't let him do what he wants is a great example. He has inevitably manufactured a rationale that allows him to avoid confronting his own personal issues.

Finally, to develop any situational strategy to address roadblocks, you must identify an approach that works in a given situation. This, as you might already have begun to suspect, is the biggest problem with general answers to problem situations. Or with suggestions from people we confide in to help us who are not in the middle of the situation.

Mr. Back Stabber

Often a passive-aggressive personality, Mr. Back Stabber is well-known in business circles. If you run into a Mr. Back Stabber, I suggest you arm yourself by reading up on passive-aggressive personalities. There's a lot to learn because there's a lot to contend with. In a nutshell, this personality type is one of the most confusing, acting out his anger or aggression literally and figuratively behind your back.

While these folks can be congenial and quite outwardly agreeable, the Mr. Back Stabbers are true snakes hiding in the corporate weeds. If you threaten him, real or imagined, he will go underground, waiting to strike and run before you know what happened. So you'll never see directly what a Mr. Back Stabber has done behind your back to sabotage you. Any anger or resentment he feels about anyone is expressed through his behavior, rather than through words.

For example, if you ask him to do something he doesn't like, he'll agree but then will procrastinate, forget to do it, constantly make excuses, or simply do a lousy job. If you disagree with anything he says in a meeting he may never confront you, but you may find the boss coming back days after a meeting questioning your response to the backstabber's viewpoint. Chances are good, when that happens, that your back stabber worked his agenda undercover with the boss. And you have a solid clue to his personality type. Needless to say, this type of behavior can create havoc in your work environment.

Some of these personality types can be even more deceiving—they can appear meek, or a bit shy in casual meetings. You might think, after first meeting them, that they are completely harmless. But, be alert; they can be masters at company politics, often rising to senior positions by killing off everyone who is, or who they perceive is, endangering their progress, typically with brilliant and strategic political backstabbing. So, when that fast-rising, easy going, non-threatening person with the soft and welcoming smile first undermines you, be particularly alert for indications that could signal a down and dirty passive-aggressive personality.

KEY INSIGHT: Never underestimate a true passive-aggressive personality in pursuit of career or business success. His entire waking life is devoted to undermining everyone he thinks is getting in his way so he can get ahead.

Back-stabbers love to subtly provoke you to get you to openly react in front of others. It might be something they've done behind your back that was leaked to you by one of their cohorts. Something that you're sure they did but that will be hard to prove came from them, like simply setting you up so you look bad. Let's say that a co-worker always volunteers to assist you in projects that you've been assigned by your boss. He, then, does little to assist you by avoiding or delaying meeting with you—a good sign you could be dealing with a back-stabber. Going to your boss and saying your co-worker is slowing you down is dangerous because he set up the problem and, no doubt, will have a ready answer if your boss calls both of you in to discuss your complaint—an answer that may make you look foolish. He might explain that he had critical business priorities that could not have been put on the back burner. The fact is that it was your job to get the project done, and, chances are good that you would take the full blame for delays. You were intentionally sabotaged.

In this case was your co-worker unfair? You bet...and your co-worker undoubtedly knew you'd be upset. And that you would probably react emotionally, and look foolish if the boss heard his ready and plausible explanation. So if your tendency is to emotionally act out, use that a clue to a personal roadblock that you need to address. When you don't react strategically, you easily fall into traps set up by passive-aggressive co-workers. So whenever you get caught up in feeling like reacting to what you think was unfair, be careful.

KEY INSIGHT: Expecting the business process and the people in it to always act fairly is unrealistic. If you have one fairness expectation in business, that's one too many. You must deal with what's in front of you, not what you want to be in front of you. This is a tough realization.

Your Strategy – Continuing to Learn a Process

At this stage your focus is to continue to get familiar with the process, rather than to try to definitely assess a personality disorder or eccentricity. Here, again, there's no absolute definitive answer for this situation. So, with that in mind, a good threshold strategy to consider if you encounter a passive-aggressive personality is:

DON'T openly react emotionally. Saying anything angrily or aggressively to Mr. Back Stabber directly and openly shows him that he hit your hot button. Then, he will keep pushing it in a variety of ways until you self-destruct.

Develop a game plan to end-run his behavior or diffuse his ability to disrupt your progress. And, for this, if you suspect you're dealing with a passive-aggressive personality, you'll need to do some solid homework on this personality characteristic.

Because they can be so disruptive in business, your only solution may be to cut off all dealings with him.

Mr. Negative

We've all had dealings with negative people. They work overtime at blocking their own progress and the progress of everyone else who'll listen to them. Negative attitudes are one of the foremost reason business progress is blocked. If you find you're very negative or are drawn to, or unduly influenced by, negative people, this will be a challenge to end-run. And, if it persists as you become aware of the damage it can do to you in business, this may be something you need professional guidance to resolve.

We often miss seeing when we're dealing with negative people because, typically, they seem to be consumed with getting ahead, and it's illogical to think they are self-destructive. In fact, they delude themselves with their focus on achieving, never realizing how they're unconsciously blocking their progress and the progress of others. Negative people are in career overdrive, going downhill.

KEY INSIGHT: The typical Mr. Negative often comes across as someone always able to assess the risks, but rarely offering any solid solutions for moving forward. This approach allows him to avoid making decisions, but also allows him to look smart, particularly since business decisions inevitably entail outcome risks.

Negative people often intimidate their audience by implying that "right" decisions don't have outcome risks. Nothing could be further from the truth, something many business people fail to realize. The fact is that decisions, perfect and imperfect, move you forward. When you reach a roadblock, you then re-route for success as needed. Doing nothing guarantees failure, something the negative person is most comfortable with.

People who are unconsciously negative, or who are afraid to confront the fact that they are negative, often unknowingly hire negative people as advisors as a way of coming to terms with their need to avoid risk. So, for unconsciously negative people, negative personalities perform a real service. They hand out ready excuses to steer clear of doing something they're too anxious to do. And by relying on the negative advisors, the decision maker doesn't have to accept the responsibility for his own negativity. In effect, it's a guiltless way out of taking inevitable business risks. Never forget: A negative person's sole agenda is to insure that he stays in his comfort zone—a zone of failure. And, if he has a hand in it, that those around him will do so as well.

Your Strategy – Continuing to Learn a Process

Dealing with negativity around you is a fact of life. If you think you or someone around you is negative, here are a few threshold strategy suggestions to avoid blocking your progress:

- If at all possible, avoid dealing or forming close relationships, personal or business, with negative people.
- Accept that any failure to avoid negative people is a clue to your own negativity. And if you suspect you are negative, start to accept the responsibility for determining why this is so.
- DON'T deny the possibility that you have a negative tendency if you're influenced by negative people or form relationships with negative people. This will help you put into perspective something that you need to resolve.
- DON'T blame others for throwing cold water on your ideas or goals.
- If you tend to be slightly negative, avoid making decisions when you're tired or your personal resources are otherwise low.
- Never forget that even if you're a generally positive, upbeat person, someone constantly around you that is negative will contaminate your thoughts and hamper your abilities.
- Always develop a game plan to end-run someone's negative attitude so it does not disrupt your progress. And that game plan may be to simply avoid discussing with Mr. Negative your thoughts and goals.

BREAKTHROUGH INSIGHT: Negativity is ingrained self-destructiveness that is difficult, and at times impossible, to manage.

Before moving on, let's explore your inclinations about negativity. Once again, write all your thoughts in your Development Diary as you read the following development situation.

YOUR AWARENESS DEVELOPMENT SITUATION

Assume that you are presently working as a sales manager for a Fortune 100 company. Your annual base salary is $75,000. You have been somewhat bored for the last few years; but with three children in school, you haven't wanted to rock your financial boat. A few weeks ago, however, you interviewed with a smaller company for a position as senior vice president of sales. They just called, offering you the job. The job appears to be both exciting and challenging. But the company is having financial difficulties. The salary would initially be the same as you are currently receiving, but you would receive a raise to $95,000 per year within six months if the financial condition is then stable. This would in part depend on how successfully you perform in your new sales position. If the company turns around financially, you would be in a great position career-wise. If it does not, you might be on the street looking for another job within a year. Now assume that you want to seek the advice of someone you know. Who would it normally be? Now that you've selected the person, describe his or her personality before reading further.

THE ANALYSIS

It would not be unusual for someone in this position to, consciously or unconsciously, seek out a negative personality. Did you? Be honest! If you did, this may be a clue to a negative tendency within yourself. And this, then, will give you an opportunity to unblock your potential.

The fact is that when dealing with a situation that involves risk, if we have negative tendencies we don't want to acknowledge, we tend to unconsciously seek advice from someone who in reality is negative to justify not taking a risk. And the negative person selected is viewed as simply someone always able to spot pitfalls to avoid. Then, by electing not to go forward based on someone else's advice, we masterfully avoid facing something about ourselves, or, worse yet, letting those around us believe something about ourselves, far more upsetting than taking a risk—being a negative person. Examples of this are all around us once we start paying attention.

And There are Many, Many More

The intent of this chapter was not to identify every possible personality type you may encounter, but merely to start you thinking about people around you and yourself and to bring some awareness into your business process so you can identify and develop strategies for handling people who exhibit clues that should alert you to possible progress roadblocks. The specific characteristics of a particular individual may be a clue to an underlying emotional agenda that can be destructive both to you and to the person exhibiting the trait. For example, people who are chronic stress avoiders, control fanatics, people pleasers and irrational worriers have underlying emotional agendas that can interfere with your progress. In all cases, clearly, you'll undoubtedly never know the motivation behind a surfacing personality characteristic, but that's irrelevant to your progress. What is important is that, when you identify characteristics of this nature, you stay alert to see if they could be clues to hidden agendas that could interfere with your business progress.

So, as you are now undoubtedly beginning to see, whether it's dealing with negative people or other roadblocks to your progress, your solution is to take responsibility for where you are and not blame others.

Summary

If you're not happy with your progress and unable to determine if you or someone else is actively sabotaging your business efforts or your career, the next best thing is to look for clues to hidden emotional agendas that you or the person you are dealing with honestly may have no idea are in play. Once you identify a clue, however, you have to develop a hard-nosed strategy to eliminate or end-run the roadblock. This, in the beginning of your awareness process, will take a conscious effort. Over time, however, doing what you need to do will flow naturally, particularly as you put into proper perspective all non-productive illusions, assumptions, agendas, feelings, beliefs and needs. As you become comfortable with accepting what you see, you will begin to naturally and consciously integrate the clues to aspects of yourself and others and develop strategies to progress in a way that's best for you.

Chapter 8

MANAGING PEOPLE EFFECTIVELY

Understanding Emotional Needs—A Key to Effective Management

To manage people effectively it's necessary to understand their emotional needs—and limits—as well as your own. Otherwise, you won't get the most from them and, worse yet, you'll fail as a manager. And when emotional needs aren't met or emotional limits are exceeded, business risk is created. By unintentionally humiliating someone in front of his or her peers, for example, you risk having your job, career or business sabotaged, willfully or unintentionally, by that person.

When you manage people, you are, in effect, managing their emotional needs. But that does not necessarily mean accommodating their emotional needs. The difference, of course, should be clear at this point—when needs are responsible and fit with business objectives they can be accommodated. Otherwise they should be addressed in a different manner—by an honest and mature reality-check discussion that sets proper expectations.

So how do you manage someone's emotional needs? First, by understanding how working for someone else, or a company, fits into that person's emotional makeup—his zone of comfort. Some people's needs will be apparent. For those that are not, you'll need to be alert for clues that signal those needs, needs that the person working for you may not even know himself. Some are socially universal needs and some may be individual to that particular person. A simple way to connect with the possible emotional needs of people working for you is to identify those needs within yourself.

BREAKTHROUGH INSIGHT: A quick way to assess someone's emotional needs and limits is to look at the personalities of the people he hires or associates with. Invariably, people with emotional roadblocks hire or associate with people who facilitate their emotional agendas.

Emotional Needs and Employment

Surprisingly, when you think about it, you'll realize there are many needs, other than financial, that people look for to be satisfied in the work environment. Needs that address their psychology—around which their feelings are wrapped. Emotional needs. For example, a need for a family or parental environment. Or a need to have an environment in which to share their problems and find help with solutions. Or a need to distract themselves from anxieties or other inner demons, which, in the constant stress-producing politics and other day-to-day pressures in business, are readily available.

In order to fully understand these needs, you'll be asked questions about your feelings and thoughts at various points so you can solidly identify what to look for in others. And you'll be asked to think about related situations to further your awareness development. Spend some time honestly with your thoughts. You'll benefit by doing so.

Here, as well, keep in mind that increasing your insights into the emotional aspects of business may push the limits of your comfort zone. So, if you're starting to feel some discomfort, or have any negative reactions to anything presented, you may be pushing against an emotional roadblock you need to eliminate or end-run.

So, let's kick-start your thinking about common emotional needs satisfied by the work environment. Some of what I'll discuss below are one and the same, but may appear different. And some will be discussed in the context of your feelings as a quick way for you to relate to them, understanding that your needs may not run parallel to the needs of people working for you.

Financial Survival

Everyone needs money to live, obviously. Employment is certainly a good alternative to theft--and safer. What may not be so obvious is that the need for financial survival may not always trump other emotional needs. When it doesn't, the decisions made to accommodate those needs may not be in the best financial or business interest of the decision maker or, for that matter, his employer.

So, as I pointed out earlier, a person with deep inner conflicts may put his emotional survival over his financial survival—without knowing it. For example, a sensitive financial analyst may stick to his analysis to avoid admitting he's made a careless mistake, one that may put the business at risk. People who don't feel good about themselves can react hostilely or defensively to apparent business snubs or put-downs. And, invariably, they do so before verifying whether in fact that was actually the case.

How about you? Have you ever felt excluded from the inner workings of a business by, say, not being invited to a business lunch? If so, did you take it personally and think you were not on a favored career track? Did you think about quitting? Did you do or say something that hurt you financially or in your relationships? Or at least consider doing so? Those who have hurt their career in some way, when pressed, can usually identify something emotionally destructive they did that led to a career problem.

QUICK AWARENESS DEVELOPMENT SITUATION

If your boss had a New Year's party and you were the only person on his staff not invited, how do you think you would handle it? Take a moment before reading further and write your thoughts in your Development Diary.

QUICK ANALYSIS

In a situation like this, some people would be so insulted they would immediately look for another job. Others might just slack off, possibly showing up late for work, clearly not acting in their best business interest. Many would be flat-out discouraged or depressed for weeks.

On the other hand, a secure person might simply ask his boss why it happened. It may have been an oversight. His secretary may have fouled up the invitations. And if not, finding out there is a problem by maturely discussing it could facilitate a progress-promoting solution.

Let's expand a bit more on the need for financial survival in the context of your experience so you have a solid benchmark to use in assessing people working with you. Have you ever worked for a company that was in financial trouble? If so, did you experience any momentary or prolonged anxiety about how you would get the money for things you needed or wanted if the company went under? If not, talk to someone who did. Explore how they felt. This type of situation always brings out a person's worst fears. Yet everyone involved always survives it. And, in fact, many go on to prosper beyond their wildest dreams once they've confronted reality.

QUICK AWARENESS DEVELOPMENT SITUATION

If you're currently a company employee, write your immediate thoughts down in your Development Diary about how you feel about your future financial security. Do you think you are absolutely safe and secure? If not, why not? For example, how do you feel about your promotional opportunities or your employment longevity? Do you think your boss likes you? What about your co-workers?

QUICK ANALYSIS

The point of this exercise? Merely to show how we very often fool ourselves about real job security to stay emotionally comfortable. That any conclusions we arrive at, or we should say guess at, can be comfort zone illusions. The reality is that there are too many unknown factors that could affect job security, and there is really no way to guarantee we're not going to experience disruptive challenges.

BREAKTHROUGH INSIGHT: In making career or business decisions, many fall back on the old saying that "A bird in hand is worth two in the bush." Unfortunately, this kind of thinking can drive illusions and block progress. This is not to say, in the case of the need to financially survive, that playing it safe is a mistake, but only that to believe you played it safe can be a misleading illusion that you hang onto to keep yourself emotionally comfortable. Play it safe, of course, but do so with the full awareness of what you're doing and what you're thinking.

Unfortunately, Corporate America has little choice sometimes but to roll over people in search of profits, a frightening reality for those who need an illusion of how tomorrow will be. Hanging on to a job because you feel you have security may in fact get in the way of actually finding a better opportunity.

BREAKTHROUGH INSIGHT: The key to security is knowing that no matter what happens you'll always be okay. Your own resources are all that you need, as long as these resources are not blocked by limiting inner emotional needs.

Personal Identity

Many people personally identify with the company employing them. If the company has an excellent reputation, they feel they'll be thought of highly. If it does not, they'll likely feel otherwise. There is nothing wrong with wanting to work for a company that enhances someone's personal image, as long as that is acknowledged as a need. And this need may be a clue to insecurity that may affect business progress. So, if someone working for you is enamored with your company's reputation, use that as a clue to an inner roadblock that could surface in other ways. And the same may be true for you—such as an unfair belief about yourself you're harboring that could get in your way.

As you might now suspect, it's not uncommon for some people to make employment decisions based on company reputation rather than company opportunity, often believing that reputation equates somehow to their personal value. For those, working for a well-known company makes them feel superior at, say, dinner parties. Those same people often buy very expensive cars they really can't afford just to impress others of their personal value.

I'm not suggesting that giving priority to a job opportunity with a company enjoying a great market reputation to compensate for something lacking emotionally is absolute mistake, but only that failing to recognize that such an affiliation for personal identity needs can jeopardize making the best possible career decision and can be a clue to an emotional issue that might prevent you from reaching your full potential. The same is true for people you hire. If the company's reputation suffers because, say, it falls on difficult times, those people may bail out.

BREAKTHROUGH INSIGHT: If you want to achieve your full potential, think twice about taking a job where the company identity is more important than personally achieving your potential.

Eliminating Irrational Anxieties

Working for a company can provide a sense of inner peace by eliminating irrational anxieties. For example, people who have difficulty handling problems or making decisions are less anxious when they know there are others to talk to for help. What's interesting in this case is that the causes of these anxieties are rarely justified, and are often based on unfounded self-beliefs that were never questioned.

The downside for these people is they often inadvertently limit opportunities in an effort to stay emotionally comfortable. And this is precisely the point I made earlier— some people make choices to stay in their emotional comfort zone, rather than make choices that benefit their career. Recognizing and accommodating this as a manager will pay dividends—and, properly handled, can help them grow as valued employees.

QUICK AWARENESS DEVELOPMENT SITUATION

Take a moment and write down, before reading further, any unfavorable reaction, or unsettling feeling, you may have had as you just read the comment about emotional security taking precedence over career opportunity.

QUICK ANALYSIS

If it troubled you, consider this: When someone presents an idea that challenges, or is different from, what we believe, we immediately resist it because it forces us out of our emotional comfort zone. The resistance may surface in a variety of forms, such as telling yourself the statement is absolutely ridiculous. The stronger the adverse reaction, the more likely a roadblock exists that can cause a reformatting of facts you need to think clearly.

The point here is to understand that your ability to deal effectively in the business world depends on your ability to honestly crack through every illusion that is not based in fact, even though doing so is uncomfortable. Ultimately, the discomfort will disappear and you'll be more at peace working in the world of reality.

Family Needs

Working for a company can be almost like living at home with your parents—a nine to five form of family life. The job environment becomes, in effect, a substitute family. There's a head of the household, the boss, always there to tell you what to do. And there are siblings, your co-workers, whom you can squabble with when you need distractions. Decisions are easier because they're spread among co-workers and the boss. Everybody knows their responsibilities. As a child looks to his parents for nurturing and survival, so does an employee look to his boss or bosses. When you're good, your parents pat you on the back. Your boss does the same, literally and figuratively. And the analogies go on. There is nothing wrong with that, as long as you keep everything in its perspective. It is a fact of life. And, as a manager, if you provide this, those working for you with this need will prosper—and so will you.

QUICK AWARENESS DEVELOPMENT SITUATION

Take a moment and write down in your Development Diary any thoughts that you're having about the comparison between employment and family life as a child. This may be a tough one to process, understandably.

QUICK ANALYSIS

How did you feel about the parent-child analogy? Did you say, for example, that was something you never thought about and found it easy to accept? Or were there other thoughts or feelings? Did the analogy make you feel uncomfortable in some manner? If so, take a moment to explore any disquieting feelings. Undoubtedly, they're not justified and could form the basis of a roadblock slowing your progress.

One more point: If you're self-conscious about the thought of being in an environment where you're, in effect, the child, be honest about it. This will allow you to gain a meaningful perspective. Working for a company does not put you in a child-like position, unless you make it so. So, if you're unsettled by the comparison, use it as a clue to something within you that you no longer need and that could be roadblocking your progress.

This particular exercise, as with the others in this book, is geared toward eliminating unfounded beliefs and illusions, as well as uncovering motivations that could be blocking your progress as employee.

Along the same line, many corporate employees dream about having their own business, but never act on it for the very reason just discussed—they don't want to leave home. They have a strong, and often unconscious, need to be in a parental or family-like environment. Again, there is nothing wrong with that, so long as it's honestly acknowledged in making career decisions. Otherwise it's easy to make a potentially limiting business choice.

BREAKTHROUGH INSIGHT: When people work for others, it's not unusual for them to have a severe attacks of the "what ifs" when they think about going into their own business. What if this happens? What if that happens? They talk themselves out of leaving, possibly missing a good opportunity. The "what if" anxiety is often an excuse to avoid moving out of their comfort zone. Going into their own business is like "leaving their family". And that's the real personal challenge that should be addressed—in effect, letting go of so-called security, real or imagined.

Acceptance

We all want to be accepted by others. That's how we were socialized from childhood—before we even knew how to fully evaluate why and to what extent it was important, if at all. When we were accepted by our parents, we were happy. When we were rejected, we were unhappy, sometimes even frightened. The same is true when people work for a company. To be accepted, we have to please the boss—the parental figure. When we don't, we risk being fired or missing a promotion or a raise. So, to keep those working for you well-motivated, you must let them know they're accepted. And if doing so threatens you, or makes you uncomfortable, use that as a clue to an inner roadblock limiting your potential as a manager.

For those needing acceptance, being fired is the ultimate rejection. For some it's humiliating and for others it's totally devastating. The world around them jumps to the conclusion that they were fired because they were no good, so they think. A sad, but often true, perception. Unfortunately, what others think to these people is often more important in determining personal worth than true value.

BREAKTHROUGH INSIGHT: When you place your personal value in the hands of others, you're risking business suicide. Competitive, jealous, resentful, and angry people are all around. They stand ready, consciously or unconsciously, to undermine everyone else's confidence through criticisms, snubs and other belittling actions. So if your personal self-worth depends on what other people think, your potential in business is at risk.

So, again, once you become aware of a particular emotional need within yourself such as the need for acceptance, use it as a clue to something within you, which, if not fully acknowledged consciously, may lead you astray in business. Being aware of a need for acceptance within yourself as an employee is the beginning of uncovering how you may have adopted false premises on which you base your self-worth. You must come to believe that you have value. Only then can you be assured that it will not be unfairly damaged by someone else. And, so, as a manager you must be aware of, and carefully manage, needs of this nature in the people working for you. If you do so with maturity and kindness, they will respond with loyalty and dedication.

Summary

To manage effectively, you need to accommodate within reason the emotional needs and limitations of those working for you, or else you risk business progress roadblocks. It's particularly important for you as a manager to be aware of the emotional needs that you want accommodated in the work environment so you can relate to and manage others well. Always remember, that there is nothing wrong with your employees having emotional needs that must be accommodated in the work environment. And there is nothing wrong with accommodating your emotional needs as a manager; as long as you're aware of them and that you factor them into your business choices and decisions. For example, if you felt ignored by your boss, or your employee reacted because he thought you ignored him, deal with it evenly and maturely. In the case of your boss, don't react out of anger or hurt feelings. And in the case of your employees, don't criticize them for being what you might think of as silly. If you do, it will cripple your progress.

Chapter 9

HANDLING ROADBLOCKING EMPLOYEES

Self-Destructive Employees Block Progress

When we are fully engaged in trying to get ahead, we often miss obvious clues that signal a co-worker or subordinate is undermining our efforts, for reasons you now know. When emotional needs are not aligned with business objectives, business progress and fairness are irrelevant.

BREAKTHROUGH INSIGHT: When someone you've worked with for a long time surprises you by doing something counterproductive, that's your clue you may be unconsciously filtering out his destructive inclinations—and, possibly, yours as well.

To increase your awareness of people who might block progress, let's explore some behavioral traits destructive people exhibit. These are traits that may not, at this stage, immediately alert you to look for potentially broader self-destructive inclinations. These aren't meant to be psychologically correct or all-inclusive; they're merely relatable lay categories that will help get you thinking about people in a way you may never have thought about before.

Failure-Prone Employees

Have you ever worked with someone who always did something for no apparent reason that drove you to distraction? Late for work. Late for meetings. Missing deadlines. Massive typos. Or similar nonsensical acts. If so, you were working with someone with a business death wish—undoubtedly, an unconscious one. A failure-prone employee.

Failure-prone employees create one problem after another. Unfortunately, without professional help, they rarely change. Bosses who keep them around often do so to simply fulfill their own emotional needs. And, in these cases, it's likely that both are codependent personalities, subtlety, desperately and unknowingly engaged in an emotionally complex relationship that is dragging both of them down. These relationships can be like those of married alcoholics—smothering and self-limiting to create distractions for deeper inner issues too painful to openly address.

BREAKTHROUGH INSIGHT: If you work with someone who always creates problems and you've allowed the situation to continue without wondering why, consider the possibility that you may have a need for someone who, in effect, makes you feel better about yourself. Someone whose work product is clearly worse than yours. And that's your clue to an inner agenda of yours that you need to correct to progress.

Failure-prone employees sometimes portray themselves as victims. They can be deceptively manipulative, able to maximize their role as a victim and manage you as a child manipulates a parent. Simply, they make you feel sorry for them. If you end up doing their work, you feel like the White Knight when you finish. You saved the day for them, and you feel good about it! But, if you fall into this trap, this is your clue to how you may be unintentionally complicit in their behavior. So, be careful; this type of employee can easily drag you down. And any need on your part to have them around could be a need to drag yourself down.

A quick question: Are you working with someone whom you constantly complain about? If so, consider that he might be failure-prone—and if you've held onto the relationship, you might be, as well. If this is the case, consider that both of you are in an unconsciously destructive business relationship, something you should immediately start to confirm by looking for other clues. Clues such as he always makes the same mistakes and you always catch them and let others know that you did. In any event, and most importantly, be honest about your role in keeping this person around. Firing him may not be the complete answer, particularly if you didn't see why you allowed the relationship to continue. If you do fire him, your challenge will be to make sure you don't hire someone with similar qualities, something you may be inclined to do without realizing it.

BREAKTHROUGH INSIGHT: It's easy to determine if you're unduly influenced by a failure-prone employee by how you react inwardly. Do you initially feel a sense of outrage at being "bothered" with his problems? When you

---

"save" the person, do you feel it was lucky for him you were around? Would he clearly have been in trouble if you had not rescued him? If so, you may be feeding an emotional need of yours that is taking time away from more effective business pursuits.

A Strategy for Handling This Personality

If you find yourself caught in a failure-prone employee situation, explore any thoughts you have in your Development Diary. Develop some possible strategies to deal with him. Experiment with what you've learned. See what works, if anything. And what doesn't. For example, you might consider changing his responsibilities or hiring an executive coach to help you work through the problem. You might consider having an honest and open discussion with him, understanding that the discussion alone may not be enough. Problem issues with strong emotional underpinnings often cannot be resolved in a discussion. In fact, once you force yourself to stop complaining, your mind will clear and chances are good that a solution will be obvious. The bottom line: Act on the problem and solve it. Don't continue to complain, and don't allow the problem to continue without an end-game strategy. Ultimately, you may have to get out of the relationship.

Negative Employees

We've discussed the negative personality type in Chapter 7, but it is worth expanding a bit more here, because this type of individual can be the downfall of progress if you are not careful.

Negative people often gravitate toward advisory roles, as you might suspect. They love to point out all the problems, to "help you avoid risk." And, invariably, they identify risk possibilities we fear the most. But when it comes to solutions? Other than what not to do, little is offered. And when they make suggestions, they're rarely innovative. For nervous managers, however, they provide a safe rationale for not making go-forward decisions and a way to avoid taking any responsibility for their own negativity.

Negative employees, nay-sayers, come in all shapes and sizes. They take the wind out of your sails when you're trying to solve business problems, find new ways to move business forward or when you express your hopes and dreams. They invariably have an answer for everything, and it's usually a two-word answer: "Too risky." They actively roadblock progress by putting a damper on virtually every new discussion idea—unless, of course, it's theirs. Racked with anxieties, they have a need to control everything so they stay in their comfort zone.

This personality type often tries to hide his negative attitude behind oblique statements such as, "Oh, I hope it works out for you" when told about new directions or efforts you're pursuing. Ultimately, everything they say and do points to risk-avoidance or sabotage. Unrealistically, they feel any decision to move forward should only be done if the outcome is certain. What inevitably escapes them is that progress cannot be made without moving into the unknown—risking outcomes. They also fail to understand the reality of business—that there's no way to predict outcomes for actions that move you forward, particularly if it's into uncharted territory. Surprisingly, they're often intelligent, using their keen analytical ability to make you think they know how to move forward without risk. Don't buy into their risk-avoidance logic, or you'll always be as stuck as they are.

What's the real issue behind a negative attitude? While there is no one answer, more than likely it's fear. Fear of change. Fear of looking stupid. Fear of being fired. Fear of the unknown. Fear of moving out of the comfort zone. Fear of loss of control. Fear of life itself!

Negative people are often jealous of those who get ahead, never realizing that they're the sole reason they're behind. And the jealously often drives them to make sure others don't get ahead of them or flat-out fail. The unfortunate part is that negative people are often talented and could be productive if they were not emotionally crippled. For them, it's more important to feel better by holding others back than by moving forward themselves.

A Strategy for Handling This Personality

There's no simple single solution to handling a negative employee. They can be very manipulative and very competitive and block your progress at every turn—sometimes quite creatively. If you see that someone's risk-avoiding advice, couched as prudent business rationale, starts to slow you down, you may have to exclude him from the decision-making process if you want to move ahead. And when you do, expect him to act out by pouting or going totally silent on you in meetings—a form of manipulation. In any event, if you can't control someone's negative influence, he must be excluded from the decision process by, for example, making sure he doesn't dominate conversations or control situations.

Let's say you're in a key business discussion and a negative employee is throwing cold water on everyone's suggestions. Confronting him directly about his negativity is risky. It can result in an avalanche of cover-up rationale and, possibly, a personal attack on your judgments. You stand a better chance of managing his negativity indirectly. Use statements such as: "Let's have the world tell us no, rather than tell ourselves no." But, even then, be prepared. Remember, as I've said, negative people are manipulative—expect them to be visibly, but subtlety uncooperative. And be careful… they are prone to go underground and sabotage you even more at every turn. So, be alert. Ultimately, you may have no choice but to exclude them completely from the decision process.

Employees Who Never Disagree

Employees who never tell you what they really think when they disagree are likely to be unconsciously self-destructive and can inadvertently impede your business progress. This is the proverbial "Yes Man". Failing to recognize a "Yes Man," or needing one around you, is a clue to an emotional roadblock in yourself that will limit you

What's behind their yes-to-everything approach? Although it's easy to think their apparent support implies agreement, it more likely shows a reluctance to express an opinion for fear, founded or unfounded, that you, the boss, will get angry. Or expose them to criticism for dumb opinions or statements. In the case of some bosses, that fear may be justified. What the "Yes Man" never realizes is his apparent accommodating nature guarantees that he'll be limited. And what their bosses never realize is that their own progress is also held back.

A Strategy for Handling This Personality

The key to working with a "Yes Man" is helping him get comfortable enough to understand that expressing his opinion, even when it disagrees with yours, is perfectly acceptable and, in fact, welcome. But you must be consistent until he sees that a contrary opinion may be good for the business process.

Quiet Employees

Employees who never, or rarely, express an opinion or offer input can create serious problems. Typically anxious or low self-worth individuals, and often talented, they're likely to avoid mentioning problems that should be addressed. They suffer in silence, are often depressed and are clearly less productive. If they're having trouble with a customer, for example, they may not tell you. The result may in fact be the loss of a customer, a loss which could have been prevented if the problem had been addressed in a timely manner. So, don't get lulled to sleep by an employee who says little and think he has everything under control or otherwise has no issues with you, his job or the business.

A Strategy for Handling This Personality

As with the employee that never disagrees, you, as a manager, need to help these reluctant talkers get comfortable enough to talk to you openly, particularly when they encounter problems. Pointing out directly what they're doing may work, but it's usually better to slowly engage them in small talk to get them comfortable talking to you. This is usually best done one-on-one, rather than is a group setting, at least until they start to open up in group settings. Here, also, you initially must be consistently supportive and understand that the process of getting them comfortable can take a long time. But it is often worth the time investment. They will undoubtedly appreciate your support and will likely eventually blossom.

Hot-Tempered Employees

Employees who easily lose their temper are clearly problem employees. Invariably, they have personal problems too complex to address here and ones that may need professional guidance for them to learn to manage their anger. Ultimately, a hot-tempered employee shuts down open communication.

Typically, hot-tempered people don't relate well to others, and, as you would suspect, often have poor interpersonal skills. Their temper can be the way they keep people at a distance or otherwise manage painful feelings that surface when interacting with people. As with any other problem employee, if you tolerate this behavior this is your clue to an underlying roadblock within you.

A Strategy for Handling This Personality

Short of having a hot-tempered employee seek professional help, there's little you can do other than fire her to ensure your business progress is not impeded. If her problem, for example, is deep-rooted, talking to her directly about her temper rarely solves the problem; her temper is simply something she has little control over.

Passive-Aggressive Employees

This is another personality type I discussed in Chapter 7 but, again, one worth expanding on here, because with this type of individual you need to be on your toes to spot if or when he might be being silently sabotaging you.

Passive-aggressive employees come in various personality wrappers—some appear as negative people, some as glad-handers. Their passive-aggressiveness may show up as sullenness, procrastination, withdrawal from participating in the business process, resentment, stubbornness, or deliberate and repeated failure to follow through on work projects. In any event, they're clearly self-destructive and can easily create morale problems, in addition to being difficult employees.

BREAKTHROUGH INSIGHT: The first time someone does or says something destructive behind your back, this is your clue that you may be dealing with a passive-aggressive personality.

One of the biggest challenges for employers of hard-core passive-aggressive people is that these employees are likely to use the federal and state employment laws to intimidate employers who make too many demands on them. These personality types, often angry with their position in life or in business, take full advantage of these rules if things are not going to their liking.

A Strategy for Handling This Personality

For hard-core passive-aggressive employees, the best solution is getting them professional help, whether it's an executive coach or a therapist. That may not be possible, and firing them, particularly ones likely to take advantage of the employment laws, is challenging. In the latter case, you must carefully document events that surround their lack of performance or lack of participation. These folks do what they want because they know if you push them out they can use whatever rules are available in law to collect damages. They, unfortunately, do a disservice to employees who are legitimately discriminated against or otherwise treated unfairly in the workplace.

Are All Emotionally Destructive Individuals Bad for Business?

A discussion of self-destructive employees would not be complete without asking whether, in the often cut-throat business world, they might have some value in certain situations. And, interestingly, they can. But you must closely manage them carefully.

For example, a Napoleonic personality can get quick and positive results when given absolute control, as long as his pathology is in synch with the business needs. They're often brought in when a business is in crisis to do whatever is necessary to turn a business around. Firing people is a breeze. Manipulating creditors is pure joy. This is playtime! These folks go into overdrive when given free rein to do anything that gets results. And they do, regardless of the social cost to the community or to the existing employees. But, these same individuals become internally destructive once the business problem is solved. Everyone inside becomes a target when the challenge is over. They start attacking others in a variety of ways to avoid looking at themselves. Superiors are suddenly stupid and working for them becomes aggravating. They often let everyone in the company know their feelings. And, when that happens, it's time to kick them out.

So, if you're looking for a ruthless individual to pull your company out of a financial mess, consider this help wanted ad to get you what you need:

JOB OPPORTUNITY

Chief Executive Officer wanted for financially troubled company. Experience required in the electronics manufacturing industry. Unusual benefit package including stock, incentive bonus plan, and loose petty cash accounting controls. Prefer a ruthless individual who can get the job done. Any type of personality disorder a plus, with a preference for a medically documented manic-depressive personality.

Of course, you couldn't actually place an ad of that nature and expect to get results. But, don't laugh; that is the type of person many problem businesses hire without knowing it. The downside is that businesses often put up with this personality type well past his effectiveness, often because it's difficult to fire someone who did so much for the company. So, if you hire a loose cannon to help you without realizing what you're dealing with, valuable time can be lost moving the company to the next phase after he's done his job.

Summary

There are many different types of employees who create work or morale problems and block business progress, for you and for them. If you, as a manager, find you have indulged a problem employee for years, this is a signal for you to look at your own motivations and be honest about why you've put up with this situation. Clearly, as a last resort, when talking to them or getting them professional help doesn't work, problem employees should be let go.

Chapter 10

DESTRUCTIVE MANAGEMENT

Problem Managers Destroy Careers

Have you ever wondered why, considering the countless business books and courses that offer solid strategy after strategy on managing people, there are so many poor managers? Particularly when all they need to offer is the obvious: incentive, positive feedback, financial security and a feeling of pride?

So what's the problem? No doubt you know by now: Unconscious destructive emotional agendas are in play. Agendas that have nothing to do with getting the most out of the people who work for them—but rather ones that serve the manager's non-productive emotional needs. And that, for someone working for a problem manager, can be a career disaster.

So, if you're working for someone who you suspect may have a destructive emotional agenda, look for clues. If you find any, it's critical to your business well-being that you gain an honest perspective on him and, if you can't change the relationship dynamics, to find a way out.

Classic Destructive Managers

Destructive managers are walking time bombs, with control and manipulation techniques finely honed over many years. People of low ethical standards, they attempt to feel better about themselves by forcing others to their emotional knees or by making sure no one working for them threatens their well-being—real or imagined. Eventually, they cripple their own career, along with the careers of those working under them, as well as the business they're involved with.

BREAKTHROUGH INSIGHT: Destructive managers often become more domineering as they progress up the career ladder. The higher they rise, the bolder they get. Then comes the inevitable day when they cross the line. Next step, unemployment, followed, if they and their families are lucky, by some serious introspection.

How do you spot a destructive manager? Sometimes it's difficult. The easy ones are egotistical, rarely listening to or respecting anyone. By treating others with disrespect, they have, at least in their mind, put themselves in a superior role. The irony is that, as boss, they're already in the top position. But that's not enough. They must make sure everyone knows at every turn that they are smarter and more worthwhile as business people than anyone else.

Then there are the ones harder to spot. They're the smooth-talking personalities who look good on the surface but are so entrapped by their emotional conflicts that their decisions are destructive to themselves, the people that work for them and the business they're involved in. So, if your gut tells you something might be amiss or things just don't add up from a business perspective with a boss, patiently look for clues that signal destructive emotional agendas. Remember the passive-aggressive personality in Chapter 7? This could be one possibility. And be particularly alert to insights you might gain from office gossip about the boss's demeanor or tactics.

A destructive manager's style makes him feel POWERFUL and compensates for what he lacks personally. Crushing others may be his way of showing his importance to the world, a world he fears thinks little of him. After all, who but an important person could take those liberties with the lives of others? Gender is irrelevant. Women also indulge. On a short-term basis, these managers may produce results. A company in trouble can be pulled together by a hard-nosed, brutal management style. Over the long term, that's another matter—these destructive managers often take the business and, at least for the moment, the emotional and business lives of the people under them down, along with themselves.

BREAKTHROUGH INSIGHT: Destructive managers are like grade-school bullies. The grade-school bully is bigger or stronger, physically or mentally, than the rest of the kids. His emotional high comes from intimidating others to compensate for what was lacking in his life. Maybe no love at home. The same is true for destructive managers, playing on their subordinates' fears and insecurities.

Many destructive managers are angry or frightened, riddled with conflicts about who they are and what their capabilities may be. Some are chronically dissatisfied with themselves. Others are running from feelings they don't want to address, most of which have likely been irrationally carried over from childhood or bad business or career experiences. Unfortunately, no matter how well they do, nothing eliminates the feelings that drive their attitude and behavior. But they frantically try—by bullying, belittling or manipulating. Sadly, they live in constant emotional turmoil, running from inner conflicts too painful to face. Invariably, they self-destruct by doing something so obviously dumb or outlandish that their career is brought to a surprising halt, such as making a series of bad business decisions or creating unnecessary risks for their companies.

BREAKTHROUGH INSIGHT: When you see business executives who seem to have everything end up being fired or going to jail for actions that make no sense in light of what they have, you're seeing first-hand people with unconscious self-destructive agendas.

Destructive Management—A Double-Edged Sword

A bad management style hurts you, whether you're the culprit or the receiver. In either case, using or suffering under, an emotionally destructive management style is a clue to an underlying emotional issue that blocks progress. So, if you're a manager, the next time you are rude or insensitive to someone working for you, identify every thought going through your mind—like an argument at home, or a criticism from your boss. Even if you don't think there is a connection, you will undoubtedly find, by tracking these incidents and your thoughts over time in your Diary, a pattern that is hampering your progress. And, if you're the victim of a destructive manager, do the same—track your feelings and thoughts in your Diary when you're treated poorly to see how you may be indulging in situations or an environment that ultimately is personally destructive.

BREAKTHROUGH INSIGHT: If you work for someone and find yourself continually talking about how poorly you're treated, take that as a solid clue that you're emotionally trapped in a destructive work relationship. Get out of the situation as soon as possible. And make sure that you don't find another one just like the one that you are in!

The Destructive Manager Trap

A destructive manager can psychologically trap you, particularly if you've arrived on the business scene with any basic misconceptions. For example, if you've been led to believe that a rude and aggressive hotshot exemplifies what a successful manager is all about, you may not see you're being managed destructively. And, worse yet, you may think you're being treated properly. That eventually will erode your confidence, which, in turn, will limit your progress.

Destructive managers make you feel that you have shortcomings, and that your shortcomings are the only reason for your lack of progress. They browbeat you into believing that nothing you do is right, reducing you to obsessively defending yourself. If you buy into what they are saying, you're finished. Clearly, their personal style is hard for most people to cope with. While their subordinates are busy covering their whatever, destructive managers are happily devising ways to enhance their own self-esteem. Discrediting others to keep their own personal conflicts under control is first and foremost in their everyday dealings with people.

Warning: If you're a perfectionist or very self-critical, be particularly wary of being emotionally trapped by put-down management styles. Chances are good that you won't see when you're being unfairly criticized, especially if it mirrors your own self-criticism. And you'll likely be consumed with eliminating all possible criticism rather than working in your best interest, never realizing that eliminating criticism from an emotionally conflicted manager is impossible. The bottom line: A desire to do a perfect job, coupled with being too self-critical, can be potentially self-destructive because it prevents you from maintaining a balanced perspective.

BREAKTHROUGH INSIGHT: People particularly susceptible to put-down management are those who don't feel good about themselves or otherwise are insecure. They rarely see what's going on. When they do, they feel they deserve it. Some even think they're lucky to have someone keep them on the straight and narrow so they don't lose their job.

Protecting Yourself from a Destructive Manager

The best protection against destructive managers is never working for one, but that's not always possible. They exist at virtually every level of management. The real danger is not recognizing their destructive tendencies when you run into them, as I've suggested earlier. Spending years dealing with a destructive individual can waste valuable career time.

Spotting a destructive manager's style sometimes requires effort, particularly if, as I've suggested, you're hard on yourself. So, if you indulge in constant self-criticism, chances are you'll never realize the extent to which it is unfairly and irrationally holding you back, at least, possibly, until someone makes you aware of it. And, then, if it's chronic, you may need someone you trust to give you a perspective on what might be happening. If you don't and it continues, you'll put your career on hold while you fruitlessly chase approval from someone who will never give it to you—or to himself.

A THIRTY-DAY DIET TO LOSE A DESTRUCTIVE MANAGER

If you suspect that you work for a destructive manager, write your observations in your Development Diary for a period of thirty days. Write exactly what you think is happening and how you react. Do not edit or judge your thoughts. After thirty days, stop reporting in your Diary. Do not review what you have written for two weeks.

At the end of the two week period, re-read your thoughts and observations and record your immediate impressions. Don't give any thought to what jumps into your mind. Just write. If you are uncertain whether your manager's style is destructive, make a copy of your Diary observations and let someone you trust, but who does not work for the same company, read them. Ask what his immediate impressions are. Don't tell him the purpose of your exercise until after you hear his comments. If your own roadblocks are very strong, you may not see the obvious. An uninvolved person will. Only then will you see, if the situation is psychologically unhealthy, that you must do something to change the situation or you will block your progress.

A Strategy—A Chance for Personal Development

Confronting a destructive manager is risky. Chances are you won't be successful in pointing out how he's being unfair. And doing so may force him further underground in his pursuits. If there's no immediate way out for you, the best you can hope for is to cope, at least to some extent, with the abuse. So, instead of complaining, take a short-term and a long-term approach to the problem. But keep one thing firmly in mind: YOU WILL NEVER CHANGE A DESTRUCTIVE MANAGER'S

APPROACH TOWARD YOU. Acknowledging this difficult reality is absolutely necessary in order for you to deal with the situation in your best business interest. Remember, however, constructively dealing with your situation may be very difficult if you have underlying destructive tendencies. If you do, be prepared for a real challenge.

Your short-term solution is to begin to emotionally move yourself off the firing range by accepting that you're not the cause of the poor treatment. Remind yourself of this at every opportunity. Make a sign with "The Cause is not ME" on it and paste it on your bathroom mirror. Look at it every morning. This may provide some relief in managing your feelings while following through on a long-term solution, which must be to find a new job.

Since you may be stuck in the situation for a while, make the best of it to develop your emotional awareness. Try to learn something about yourself by watching how you react emotionally. If your boss hurts your feelings or makes you angry, see if the abuse prompts something you already fear is true about yourself. Most of us are hurt or get angry when a personal sore point is hit. For example, it's easy to become angry when our performance is criticized, particularly if we're insecure in our job. On the other hand, if we feel secure about ourselves, we might take the comment constructively, provided it is well-founded. The key for your awareness development is to honestly explore why you are thrown off when hearing something upsetting. Working for an abusive boss is a great way to try to reorganize your emotional side so you treat yourself fairly and to learn how to maintain your emotional equilibrium when under attack. And in this type of situation, you are under attack!

Finally, in developing your long-term and short-term strategies, use your Development Diary to track your thoughts and feelings. Such as after being criticized, do you feel you won't be promoted? Or do you feel that you'll be fired? Try to identify any thoughts that suggest you deserve to be treated poorly. All of this will help you frame the problem so you can amass your resources to put yourself back on track.

Positive Management May be a Personal Challenge

A discussion of destructive managers would not be complete without making a point about one reason a positive management may fall by the wayside. This is something that can be puzzling because it's common sense—treat others like you want to be treated yourself. And that may be the clue to why some have a put-down management style—it's possible that being treated poorly works well with their psychology. They may, for example, prefer to be emotionally abused rather than be treated with respect for a variety of reasons too complex to discuss here. And they may project that preference on the people they manage. In addition, people who feel bad about themselves often and unknowingly find it more comfortable to be in an unsupported environment that distracts them from their inner conflicts.

Expanding on this possibly leads to something I've discussed earlier—that emotional conflicts unconsciously take control of behavior and may surface as a style or approach dictated by the emotional conflicts a manager is struggling with. For example, if a manager feels insecure, he may only hire non-threatening people he can dominate—all without being fully aware of what he is doing.

There are other reasons a supportive management style may not be the style of choice. For example, a manager may have a belief about what a successful manager should be based on statements from people who may also have unfounded assumptions and illusions about effective or successful management approaches. Or he may have had a poor role model—patterning his management style after someone who he thought was a successful manager but who in fact was emotionally abusive.

BREAKTHROUGH INSIGHT: Playing a role for success can be a trap for the unsuspecting. Be yourself. And if being yourself is being a bully, your time at the bottom will come around again.

Making matters even more challenging is that, to the unsophisticated, it's entirely possible that constructive or supportive managers may look weak. And managers struggling with inner conflicts certainly don't want to appear weak. Can you imagine how humiliating it would be if anyone thought they were weak? Like the fellows at the Club? Or maybe, worse yet, that attractive assistant at the front desk?

BREAKTHROUGH INSIGHT: Effective managers feel good when people go the extra mile. They get no satisfaction from crushing people under their corporate feet. So, when you see a destructive management style, you have a clue to underlying bad feelings and emotional conflict.

If you're finding any of this hard to believe, think a moment about those whom society often glamorizes—the ruthless hotshot, the robber baron. Add to this the unfortunate fact that many business people believe that tough talking and bulldozing subordinates makes others think they're successful, and it's easy to see how a poor management style can be assumed. So it stands to reason that it can take guts to manage in a positive manner. And that can happen only when people are secure within themselves—well balanced emotionally.

QUICK AWARENESS DEVELOPMENT SITUATION

Take a moment before reading further to explore whether you feel a positive management style appears weak. Jot down your thoughts in your Development Diary. Think about what type of business leader impresses you the most. Imagine yourself as the president of a Fortune 100 company. What style would you adopt? Would you like to be thought of as a tough, outspoken, and abrasive wheeler-dealer? If so, dig deep and see if you can identify why.

QUICK ANALYSIS

This exercise is geared toward identifying unfounded beliefs and illusions that you may have about what it takes to be successful as a manager. If you think the tough-talking bully-style manager is the best, consider where that belief came from. And if it's someone you knew, was he happy? Or did you think he was happy based, for example, on the home he lived in or the car he drove? Or, possibly, was it something you read or saw on television?

Keep in mind: If any beliefs were not based on your own experience, they could be the basis of roadblocks preventing your progress. Use them as clues to unblock your full potential.

Summary

If you are working for a destructive manager, your career and talents will be jeopardized. It's essential that you stay alert to situations when this might be the case. That requires that you step back from any self-critical aspect of yourself to look at the situation more objectively. If you find that you destructively manage others, be assured that eventually, you will suffer. So, in either situation, you need to take a hard look at what is occurring and look for a short-term and a long-term solution to a destructive management style—even yours.

Chapter 11

TAKING ACTION AND MAKING DECISIONS

Make Sure Your Real Business Goal is Success

As you now know, if you're not where you want to be in business, it's highly likely your success is blocked by unconscious, and destructive, emotional needs. The good news is by honestly facing what can be a frustrating, and even frightening, possibility, there's something you can do about it.

As you also know, unproductive emotions and feelings so control some situations that business failure or financial loss is irrelevant. As you begin to consider this as a possibility, you'll clearly see that people filled with anxiety or other emotional discomfort invariably act to relieve their discomfort at the expense of their best business interest. Although beyond the scope of this book, the same is true in personal relationships.

A classic but extreme example of irrational feelings taking absolute control is when people have temper tantrums. The explosive anger, a reaction to something aggressively challenging their coping mechanism, short-circuits their ability to see the consequences of their foolish and personally destructive anti-social behavior. Ultimately self-destructive, uncontrolled anger destroys business, and personal, well-being. But the same can be true on a much more subtle and unconscious emotional level with self-destructive tendencies surfacing in ways not so readily apparent—a challenge you could be facing when you're not where you want to be in business and don't know why.

BREAKTHROUGH INSIGHT: Reacting angrily to upsetting situations is not in your best business interest, unless it's calculated, and, even then, it's risky. Calmly and directly expressing your feelings puts you in control and is in your best business interest.

A good example of when more subtle disruptive, and irrational, feelings derail productive relationships often occurs in business partnerships. People who work together must interact well for the business to work. When uncontrollable and unproductive feelings take over, the business can be crippled or destroyed. A partner's rude behavior may bring an end to a viable business when the other partners can no longer tolerate it if they react emotionally, for instance, by refusing to include him in meetings, rather than strategically looking for an effective solution. When feelings take over, it's often no longer possible, without intervention, to systematically and rationally address and solve business relationship problems. Emotional needs come first, and business viability drops by the wayside—to everyone's detriment. On the other hand, by keeping feelings under control, an offended partner has a solid chance of resolving conflicts to his personal benefit.

Examine and Re-Examine All Reasons Behind Your Goals

To succeed, honestly and periodically re-examine what you tell the world and yourself you want in business, whether it's a top management position, a good career track, a worthwhile, fulfilling and interesting job, financial security or something else. And that means each time you examine your goals taking a hard look at why you think you don't have what you want. Rarely does that fault lie with anyone but you.

What we think or tell the world and ourselves we want can be very different than the dictates of our controlling unconscious and unproductive emotional agendas. When there's a disconnect between our conscious goals and what we need to remain emotionally comfortable, success roadblocks occur. A good example is someone who has a compulsive need to be right or dominate everyone he comes in contact with and who also has high career goals. The need to be right or dominate, driven by inner emotional conflicts, is how he copes with his inner demons. Unfortunately, both are offensive to others and can block progress. What's interesting is that the mere setting of the goal in his mind is the elixir to all inner turmoil. In effect, he has deluded himself into believing that the cause of his inner turmoil is lack of success. But, what's even more fascinating is that if this type of person reaches his goal, he often rushes to find another all-consuming goal or activity, not realizing that doing so is, in effect, an unconscious inner coping mechanism that distracts him from painful feelings. And he might end up acting out inappropriately in his personal life in a way that ultimately affects his business success, such as drinking heavily or openly cheating on his spouse.

Accept That Emotions Control as a Fact of Business Life

As I've suggested, career and other business decisions can be driven by counterproductive emotional needs that roadblock success. They could be yours or the needs of those around you. The hard truth is that, realistically, there's often little, if anything, you can do about unproductive emotionally-based decisions others make that block progress. But the good news is that there is never a time when you cannot move yourself forward, provided you've make a commitment to always act in your own best business interest.

BREAKTHROUGH INSIGHT: If you honestly acknowledge and willingly accept all of your feelings, there'll never be a day when you won't see when what you or others think or do may be tainted by emotional agendas that serve no purpose other than to manage anxieties, fears and other inner discomfort.

One of the biggest mistakes we make in business, when we're unaware of our own emotional needs and anxieties, is basing our decisions on how we think someone will react to what we say or do. When we don't connect with what's driving our belief, invariably and without realizing it, we incorrectly assume people will act or think based on what we think they will think or do. If, for example, we're negative or otherwise self-destructive and we're not fully in touch with our nonproductive agendas, we read that into others—we, as the psychologists say, project our thoughts onto others. And we do it automatically and unconsciously.

Projection is a psychological concept easy to understand intellectually, but very difficult to relate to emotionally. Simply, it's that we act or think based on the movie we're projecting on the screen of life in our mind.

Why we project inner thoughts or feelings onto others is complex and beyond the scope of this book. But, simply, one explanation is that our manufactured self, our ego, sees our misguided thoughts or feelings somewhere and what is referred to as our super ego alerts our ego to possible punishment and it immediately jumps into action and causes these thoughts or feelings to be imposed on someone else to avoid seeing something upsetting within our own self.

So, in a nutshell, our projections are, in effect, a way of distancing ourselves from what may be our dysfunctional characteristics, so we can examine or comfortably manage them by believing they are outside of us. If you don't like someone, for example, but feel you should like everyone, you might project onto him that he doesn't like you, which, in turn, allows you to avoid him as well as cope with your not liking that person.

BREAKTHROUGH INSIGHT While the explanation of projection is one commonly accepted, keep in mind that beliefs or theories offered, such as the ones about projection that cannot be determined or verified within your own experience, should not be necessarily taken as absolute truths. But they should never be dismissed offhand when they come from apparent credible sources. That said, whether the theory offered by traditional psychology is correct or not is irrelevant. All that matters is that you begin to look for ways that you may be blocking yourself, and the concept of projection is something easy to relate to—at least from a result viewpoint. So, as stated in the beginning, look to your own experience to validate the benefits of what you're being told—by anyone, including the author.

A woman physically attracted to a male co-worker unable to cope with her feelings might accuse the co-worker of flirting or making sexual advances, even though the co-worker did not—a projection. Similarly, a man cheating on his wife might think (project) that she's cheating on him to manage his feeling of guilt. Another, but extreme, example would be when someone who hates himself universally projects that everyone hates him—a common attribute of paranoia. Very simply, projecting converts moral or neurotic anxiety into reality anxiety, something most of us are more comfortable addressing.

BREAKTHROUGH INSIGHT: When dealing with people in business, if we're not careful, our projections can mislead us because we actually and quite honestly believe that someone we're dealing with thinks or feels in a particular way about us, not realizing that this is in fact how we think or feel about him.

So, an interesting, but sometimes uncomfortable, way to get insights into your real self is to consider the possibility that any characteristics or values you believe, but don't know for a fact, someone you just met has, might be characteristics or values that you have—your assumptions about that person simply being a projection of how you really are. Doing so will help you eliminate thoughts and feelings that actually get in your way. Say, for example, you just met someone and immediately feel that he's honest. As soon as you have that thought, acknowledge that this impression may be the result of a projection of your own honest inclinations. By keeping that possibility in mind, it's less likely that you'll put your guard down and miss clues to any possible dishonesty on his part. So, the key to working effectively with people is to always be aware of the possibility that you could be projecting any of your good or bad feelings about yourself onto them.

BREAKTHROUGH INSIGHT: Use your projections to your advantage by honestly confronting destructive possibilities within yourself that you may only be able to see when you look at others.

Let's look a little closer at how projections can block business progress. Assume you withdraw emotionally when pressured for a decision or are pulled into an emotionally charged discussion. The psychologists would call you a distancer, someone who keeps people at a distance by, say, clamming up. Now assume that you've been working as an engineer, but decided to take a sales job in an effort expand your opportunities. So, for example, if you don't like to receive, or be pressured by, marketing calls, you could well assume that other people feel the same way, and each time you pick up the phone to make a sales call that could create undue anxiety. So much so that you may find a variety of rationalizations not to make the call, and sabotage your sales career.

QUICK AWARENESS DEVELOPMENT TEST

Take a moment before reading further and write in your Development Diary all the thoughts now running through your mind, regardless of what they are.

QUICK ANALYSIS

Did you catch yourself feeling a bit uncomfortable or feeling like you wanted to put the book down and stop reading? How about any other thoughts or feelings that might suggest some form of rationale as to why the projection discussion may not apply to you? Or that the concept is silly? If so, any of these could be clue as to how you could be derailing yourself without realizing it. But don't be hard on yourself. We're all in the same boat, operating under the same illusions, misconceptions and psychological eccentricities.

In a nutshell, to eliminate projections that block your progress, consider as a possibility that you may be projecting your thoughts or feelings when you see others or the world in a favorable or an unfavorable way. And always keep in mind, for example, when people are criticizing you, that their criticism may well be a projection of their own criticism of themselves. In that case, you might suggest to them what they might be doing—but be careful. Doing so can be a quite a shock and will often be met with emphatic, and even aggressive, denial.

Armed with this new awareness sensitivity to what you may be doing, be assured that you have another powerful tool to use to strip away all illusions and misconceptions that slow you down. But, in the beginning, be prepared to feel uncomfortable, disappointed, helpless and even sad at times. These are natural feelings as you adjust to the way things are as opposed to the way you think things are or should be. These disconcerting feelings will pass. And, in fact, you will find that you will have a new sense of power and control—power that is naturally within you.

Take Control of Your Future—Acknowledge Business Reality and Trust Your Gut

It's hard to believe that unconscious emotional issues can unknowingly move a decision in a destructive direction, but it happens every business day. If you have any doubts, start paying attention to how the decisions by people around you are being made. See if you can spot one situation in which an overriding emotional inclination is steering the business decision the wrong way. Initially, it may be difficult because emotional motivations are carefully covered with business logic. And your belief system, and projections, may be filtering out or distorting what's actually in front of you, particularly, as you now know, if you've had a preconceived notion that the business process is not controlled by emotional agendas. But as soon as you spot one, you'll be amazed at how your view of the business process will start to change.

BREAKTHROUGH INSIGHT: Each time you suspect an overriding emotional undercurrent has taken over the decision process, make note of it in your Development Diary. Keep track of what happens. Record all your impressions. As certain ones prove correct, you'll learn to hone your detection skills. As you see the emotional process in others, you will learn to catch underlying inclinations within yourself that may not fit your best business interest.

One more important point: Going forward, also use your gut instincts to help guide the way. If you suspect a decision is based on someone's emotional agenda trust your gut and dig deeper to ensure the decision makes business sense. That suspicion is your first clue that something could be amiss. Don't second-guess yourself simply because you're initially relying on your instincts. Trust them. In doing so, however, understand that although they're always accurate, they may not always be so for reasons that first pop into your mind. So, don't act on them until you have confirmation of what they seem to be telling you. Remember here as well, your interpretation of what you think your instincts are telling you could be colored by your own projections or mistaken beliefs.

QUICK AWARENESS DEVELOPMENT TEST

Have you ever felt a business suggestion made by a boss or someone you work with was primarily motivated by personal rather than dollars and cents reasons? Such as a suggestion to buy new office furniture to impress customers? Or a proposal for a new business acquisition in an area of the country he'd enjoy visiting—like sunny California?

We're all guilty of doing this from time to time. It's easy to blur the line between personal and business reasons, and to do it without fully being aware of what is happening. So, let's examine this possibility for you.

Assume that you were asked to explore new acquisition opportunities in San Francisco or Detroit, which place would you pick? Would your decision be based strictly on where the best business opportunity was? If you picked California, any guesses about when those trips would be scheduled? Would you be in and out quickly during the week or planned around a weekend? Be honest. Write your thoughts in your Development Diary.

QUICK ANALYSIS

Your answers may show that you are strictly profit-oriented. Then again, you may find that there would be some personal reasons to direct your explorations to a personally more palatable location. The point here is to learn to recognize what you're doing, so your decision is made with all factors in consideration and you don't lose sight of your business needs.

Common Emotional Issues that Drive Bad Decisions

As I've discussed, business decisions that satisfy unproductive feelings can be bad for you and the business you're in. In Corporate America, for example, many well-meaning decision makers act to protect their job security and their salary and bonus first and the profitability of the company a far distant second. When that happens, obviously, the company can suffer.

So, let's look at some common types of emotional undercurrents that can lead you or people you're working with or for down the wrong path.

Anxiety-Driven Decisions

Making decisions to avoid anxiety will roadblock success, something many do without realizing it. Unfortunately, anxiety is a fact of business life, so it must be accepted. So, as I've suggested, your best business strategy is to always keep your anxieties in proper perspective. And that means to hold on and live with them, rational or irrational, so you don't cripple progress. If you can't, this is your clue that unproductive and unconscious feelings could be damaging your business well-being.

Assume, for example, that you just took on a new product in your business and it's not selling well. In the process of taking on this product you increased your overhead, which was nerve-racking. You have two basic choices. Stop selling the product and cut your overhead back to relieve your anxiety. Or live with the anxiety of an increased overhead and see if you can determine another strategy to boost sales. Other possible factors aside, a decision to dump the product may eliminate a good business opportunity.

Any overreaching need to be anxiety-free in business is simply an emotional coping mechanism that may not serve your business best interest. Bumps in the business road inevitably create anxiety. So, when anxiety surfaces, your challenge is make sure you don't inadvertently sabotage progress simply to cope with, or eliminate, anxiety. Very simply, your ability to get positive results in business depends on recognizing when a coping mechanism may result in a counter-productive business behavior, one that serves no purpose other than a way to feel personally comfortable. So, particularly when you feel the urge to emotionally act out, dig deep and put power back into your business life by being honest about what you're really trying to achieve. By keeping a clear business perspective, you're less likely to make decisions that keep you emotionally comfortable, but don't move you forward.

BREAKTHROUGH INSIGHT: Acknowledging the possibility that we're often controlled by our irrational anxieties enhances our awareness development process and makes a positive business path easier.

Being sensitive to when anxieties may be the basis for decisions others are making can result in better business results. If, for example, you suspect that someone's decision may be geared to avoid personal anxiety, depending on your relationship, it may be possible to eliminate a potential progress block by merely pointing that out. But, no matter what your relationship, do it tactfully…for obvious reasons. And suggest it as a "possibility", not a fact.

This was made clear to me a number of years ago. I was participating in the startup of a newsletter publishing business, and marketing the newsletter cost-effectively was a key threshold issue. The person handling the daily publishing operation, John, was a new and very capable addition to the publishing group. It was suggested during one of the initial meetings that he market the newsletter using some highly directed press releases. John, with a heavy direct mail background, felt direct mail should be used first and then, as that developed, use directed press releases. Other factors aside, the founders generally found the best way to start any business was to take advantage of all marketing avenues. After some discussion, John still resisted the press release suggestion, even after the group pointed out what everyone thought was obvious—he had nothing to lose by using all channels available. I asked John if there could be any possibility that he was in any way uncomfortable about using press releases for any reason. John said absolutely not and flatly maintained that he thought they weren't a good idea. The group decided to break for lunch at a local restaurant.

At lunch everyone talked about local and national news events. John started to relax and feel included. After lunch, one group member asked John whether there could be a possibility that he was resisting press releases because he would rather do what he was most personally comfortable with, quickly adding that he could be completely wrong. John opened up and acknowledged some anxiety about pursuing what, for him, was an unfamiliar marketing direction. Once his underlying issue came to the surface, an easy solution was suggested—get someone involved who knew about press release marketing. John then became enthusiastic about increasing the chance of success by expanding the marketing effort.

BREAKTHROUGH INSIGHT: In order to identify, point out and clear away emotional blocks in a group situation, first establish a non-threatening environment. The objective should always be to ensure no one feels inadequate, weak, afraid or otherwise unable to measure up.

Frustration-Based Decisions

Many people block business progress by giving up as soon as they become frustrated, when the going gets tough or their hoped-for outcome take too long. In a sense, this is understandable. When everything comes to a tumbling halt, when plans go astray or when the pursuit of the goal seems endless, all sorts of bad feelings surface—the causes of which are often hidden from our awareness—such as depression or panic. So, if you run into a business speed bump and start to say things like what you're working on is not worth the effort, use that as an immediate clue to dig deeper into inclinations that are nothing more than ways to cope with uncomfortable inner feelings. In these cases, your strategy should always be to persist unless you hit a brick wall in which case you should re-route. But certainly not give up.

BREAKTHROUGH INSIGHT: A constructive approach in business requires constant effort and an ability to cope with the unknown. A negative or destructive approach is virtually effortless and anxiety-free. Think about it.

A classic example of giving up when a business roadblock occurs is the would-be entrepreneur who runs into trouble in his first startup attempt and then immediately gives up and looks for a job. If, instead, he had taken a close and honest look at what went wrong and tried again, avoiding the earlier mistakes, his chance of success would have improved. If things still didn't work, re-examining the second effort and making adjustments again would increase the chance of success. To do this, however, requires emotional honesty and the willingness to cope with the anxiety of not knowing whether he's capable of getting his business off the ground.

BREAKTHROUGH INSIGHT The challenge for success is always to live with uncomfortable, and possibly devastating, inner feelings, so that you can keep moving forward.

So, if you find yourself in a situation where you feel like "bailing out", use this as a clue to something within you that is blocking your progress. And something that can be eliminated or end-run using the insights and strategies I've provided, and your own common sense.

BREAKTHROUGH INSIGHT: There's no magic to getting what you want in business—it takes time and trial and error effort. Unfortunately, too many of us have been taught that success depends on luck, extreme intelligence or something else that we may have not have, rather than simple perseverance. Finding success is like solving any other problem. There's an answer if you keep looking. And you can only keep looking if you keep your destructive emotional mechanisms under control.

Is the Project Your Baby?

Falling in love with a project or an idea can derail true success. Once they are emotionally attached, some people become so preoccupied with completing the project or fulfilling their idea, they lose sight of business realities and re-routing needs or opportunities.

So, when you become preoccupied with a particular project or idea, use it as a clue to an emotional need that may hamper an honest assessment of what you should be doing to progress. Hanging onto something for no good reason other than because it was your idea may be a way you try to validate your perception of yourself or your reality. Doing so is not the correct business strategy for success.

So, if a project idea becomes nothing more than a way of saying, "Look at how innovative I am," and you can't see that's really driving you, you may miss where real opportunity lies. Being an honor student, for example, is a solid objective. It can open many doors. On the other hand, a student pursuing that goal to make himself feel smart may not be addressing the real issue driving the need, which is that he does not feel smart. Getting on the honor roll will not solve that problem. It may be a temporary fix, but eventually another one will be needed.

QUICK AWARENESS DEVELOPMENT EXERCISE

When a project is "your baby," put down all your thoughts in your Development Diary, even those that seem irrelevant. Then ask these questions and jot down the answers:

- Why are you pursuing the project?
- What does it mean to you personally?
- How will you feel if it succeeds or fails?
- What do you think your co-workers, friends or family members will say if it succeeds or fails?
- How do you think you will appear to your co-workers, family or friends if it succeeds?
- Are you trying to show others how creative or smart you are? And if so, do you think that your project will make a long-term and convincing impression?

QUICK ANALYSIS

The purpose of this exercise is to see if you can identify what your real needs are when the project is your baby. Once you do, you can determine whether these needs will actually assist your business pursuits. For example, will it move you forward as fast as you wish? If not, re-think the basis of your project. If, on the other hand, satisfying an emotional or intellectual need is of primary importance, you may have to compromise your business career. Recognizing what is most important to you eliminates any inclination to satisfy needs others have placed on you. The key is to avoid pursuing goals that will ultimately have little real meaning for you.

Our Way of Experiencing Others May Create Blocks

The way we were taught to evaluate what may be the meaning of what people say or do can block progress. As I've suggested earlier, invariably, well-meaning teachers and mentors offer guidance based upon their own beliefs. When these beliefs are colored by their emotional needs or agendas, they may be faulty. Or they may simply be wrong for what you hope to achieve.

BREAKTHROUGH INSIGHT: Be very careful about accepting at face value business guidance from anybody who has not achieved what you want to achieve.

It could well be based on beliefs that have no relevance to your efforts and could send you down the wrong path.

Always keeping in mind the possibility that someone's business advice may be tainted by unconscious and destructive emotional needs will keep your thinking for business clear. And it will increase your ability to see and end-run patterned roadblocks created by the artificial rules of others which can get in your way. This may take some effort at first—it's no easy task to change the way you have been taught to think in business. But the effort will pay dividends.

QUICK AWARENESS DEVELOPMENT TEST

If a business associate or boss did not return your telephone call for two days, how would you feel if, when he returned the call, he gave no excuse for the delay? Would you feel insulted? What about other feelings? See if you can identify one very remote feeling. Write your thoughts in your Development Diary before reading further.

QUICK ANALYSIS

If you think you would be angry or feel insulted, this could be a clue to inner feelings that can be blocking your progress. Simply, how you experience what he did might be an incorrect assumption that might cause you to act self-destructively.

There's nothing wrong with having any uncomfortable feelings as long as you're aware of what they are and, if possible, why they exist. Remember, as I've said, typically, unsettling feelings come from childhood or early business memories that may no longer have a place in your life. And if you act on the basis of these feelings you may not be acting in your best business interest.

BREAKTHROUGH INSIGHT: If you have trouble taking time to write your thoughts in your Development Diary, or otherwise taking note of them, that may be a clue to something within you that could be blocking your progress. If you can't make the effort, explore why. It will help.

A good example of progress blocks that can occur when we incorrectly experience what we think others are personally saying to us happens to sales people who "cold" call to generate business leads. When repeatedly rejected, many become "phone shy," unable to make further calls. They take the rejection personally. On the other hand, those who don't take the rejections personally can be effective cold callers. By keeping their perspective, they're able to see that the problem is not something personal, but rather one that needs revisiting to overcome. They're challenged to find an answer. Perhaps the product they're offering is not right for the market they're calling. Perhaps their pitch is not effective enough. In any event, because they don't feel they're the problem, they don't give up.

Let's now explore how your interpretation of why people are reacting in a particular way can create success blocks. As you're reading the following situation be aware of your thoughts and make a note of them in your Development Diary before reading the Analysis.

YOUR AWARENESS DEVELOPMENT SITUATION

Assume you're the Director of New Business Development for a shoe manufacturing company. When you returned from lunch, you found a telephone message on your desk stating that the president of your company, Mr. Johnson, called while you were out. The message read for you to call Mr. Johnson as soon as you got back from lunch and went on to say that he needed to discuss the implications of a major acquisition before he commits the company. You know he's considering you and another department head to fill a high-paying senior staff position.

How do you feel about the opportunity to give your input to Mr. Johnson? Do you feel your chances for career success are enhanced? Have you ever been in a similar situation? If so, how did you feel? Before reading further, write in your any thoughts down in your Development Diary.

Now assume that you called Mr. Johnson back at two o'clock p.m. and learned he was out of the office. His secretary, however, said that she would let him know you called. He was expected back in ten minutes. Five o'clock came without a call from Mr. Johnson. You went to the office early the next day to be available in case Mr. Johnson called. Noon came and went without a call. At twelve thirty p.m. you headed for the cafeteria. On your way, you saw Mr. Johnson in the hallway. You walked over and asked him how the acquisition was progressing. He hurriedly told you everything was fine. He mentioned nothing about his telephone call to you yesterday. After a few moments you asked whether you could be of assistance and whether the concern he had conveyed in the telephone message was still an issue. He abruptly said "No." He then added that he had taken care of it himself and hurried off.

THE ANALYSIS

- If you haven't already addressed the issues raised by the following questions, do so now in your Development Diary.
- Do you think you missed an opportunity or that Mr. Johnson could have been unhappy with you, possibly, because you were unavailable when he called?
- How would you feel if someone else had helped him resolve the matter?
- Would you think you were edged out by another employee?
- Did you have any thoughts that your opinion may not have been valued by Mr. Johnson?
- Did you consider the possibility that the issue had simply been a non-issue and you were not needed for assistance?
- Can you see how your reactions could depend solely on what you thought may have happened?
- Did you realize that what you thought could be influenced by what you generally expect certain actions or responses to mean?

Most of us work constantly, and unconsciously, at trying to change the people around us to avoid our own anxieties. And, for success or happiness in business, that is an absolute waste of time. If, instead, we worked at reprogramming our thinking, rather than trying to orchestrate the outside world, we would move forward—constantly. So, if you don't feel secure about yourself, situations like the one described in the last exercise can easily be interpreted as a personal slap in the face. And, if you're not fully in control of your feelings, it's possible that you may subtly, or even openly, act out your feelings in a way that sends a wrong message. This is an easy trap many fall into when feelings take over. Unfortunately, unless we're constantly aware of our emotional motivations, inner conflicts can push us in a destructive direction.

Don't Try to Be Right

A need to be right can distort your ability to make good business decisions. And once a decision is made, the same need can block or distort seeing re-routing changes that may be necessary as the process plays out. Adding fuel to the fire, that same need can completely eliminate any chance of success.

QUICK AWARENESS DEVELOPMENT EXERCISE.

Have you ever told someone that you knew how to solve a problem or make something happen and then been unable to do it? If so, was it embarrassing to admit you couldn't do it? What about any other feelings?

QUICK ANALYSIS

If you've had this kind of experience, great. All that is important here is to increase your sensitivity to how your feelings can disrupt your ability to have a business success.

A self-imposed need to be right is a clue to an inner conflict that can disrupt progress. Your focus should be on succeeding, in whatever form it takes. Trying to figure out the perfect course of action is nothing more than creating an illusion to get emotionally comfortable. You can't predict what will happen, unless, as I've said, it's failure and you have a hand in it. Success is something quite different than being right about what you say you will do.

BREAKTHROUGH INSIGHT: Society idolizes people who can seem to predict outcomes. Doing so is yet another illusion many use to calm anxieties. Unfortunately, a preoccupation with predicting outcomes can create unnecessary and unrealistic success objectives. Business requires flexibility. It's completely foolish to concern yourself with whether what you initially thought would happen does actually happen in the way you said it would.

Unfortunately, business schools and Corporate America make a meal out of believing that the "right" course can be set before you start. And if you've bought into that belief, you've been misled. People who make it big understand that success in fact is an intuitive and trial and error re-routing process layered over with common sense and clear and experienced thinking. So, notwithstanding all the business school rationale and analysis tools, the business process is merely a game of intelligently getting into action and then re-routing until you get results that benefit you, and not necessarily the results that you thought you would get.

QUICK AWARENESS DEVELOPMENT EXERCISE.

Take a moment and write the first thoughts that come to mind in your Development Diary about the success process statements made in the preceding two paragraphs. Hold back nothing. Disagreement. Outrage. Anger. Feeling depressed or discouraged.

QUICK ANALYSIS

Some of the statements that were made are contrary to established business thinking. A strong adverse reaction to any may be a clue to ingrained beliefs that may be getting in your way.

Success in the business process requires flexibility and openness to uncertainty, with the confidence that solutions and success are possible, but maybe not in the manner anticipated at the beginning of the process. Unfortunately, when you're working for others who have ingrained beliefs, particularly if they're not entrepreneurial or have spent their entire business life in a sheltered business environment, your ability to move forward in your organization may be dependent on your ability to accurately predict what will happen and when it will happen. This is difficult to do, at best. And when new approaches or directions are involved, it's more likely unrealistic. If it happens as predicted, consider yourself lucky.

If you're struggling with these suggestions, it may be that they're taking you out of your belief comfort zone. If so, consider them as possibilities without drawing any conclusions, and start to look for ways to personally verify whether they're true for you. If you're not where you want to be in business, clearly it's time to start re-thinking how you view business and its process.

So, when we become preoccupied with having made the "right" decision, we're apt to handle problems along the way with a view to achieving what we originally planned. And that may lead us astray. The key to ultimate success is to be less concerned with predicting the outcome we planned and more concerned with finding success. Even a wrong action can lead us in an opportune direction. Opportunities are based on what actually exists, not on what we would like to think exists. Don't be the person with an answer in search of a problem. Be the person who found a problem in search of an answer.

BREAKTHROUGH INSIGHT: In business, you must work to fit the market needs, not try to work to fit your needs into the market.

The Way You Think Things Should Be Can Trap You

Thinking that a person or the marketplace should logically perform in a particular way can cause you to miss opportunities. Your logic is based on your inner assessment process. And it may be colored by obscure emotional needs, particularly if you have any unconscious self-destructive issues that you have neither identified nor resolved. Very simply, emotional roadblocks can create faulty logic.

BREAKTHROUGH INSIGHT: If a successful business person offers you advice that doesn't seem logical, look for clues in yourself that underlying destructive emotional issues may possibly be creating faulty logic.

Summary

In making business decisions, you must always be on the alert for hidden emotional needs within yourself that can lead you astray. Unfortunately, many business people make decisions without having the remotest idea of their emotional needs or limitations. It may not be possible to take into account all emotional issues that may drive a business decision, but with increased awareness you'll be less likely to make decisions on the basis of a destructive emotional need. The real danger is when emotional undercurrents block your ability to see facts which would lead your decision in another and more productive direction.

Chapter 12

CLEAR-THINKING STRATEGIES FOR BUSINESS

A Few Clear-Thinking Strategies

To identify roadblocks to business progress, whether they are your own or those of people around you, so you can develop effective strategies to move yourself forward, you must clear any anxiety or other mental static interfering with finding roadblock solutions. As I've discussed, if your mind is filled with thought static, finding solid solutions is difficult, if not impossible.

There are two techniques you can use to clear thought static. One is to bring your awareness into the current moment, something I'll refer to as becoming present through a mechanical change in your physical actions. Bringing yourself into the moment, sometimes called present thinking, clears past and future thoughts that might be consuming and polluting your problem-solving ability. When you're present, you can fully focus on the challenge in front of you and find the most effective course of action.

You can also clear thought static by using a relaxation and visualization technique, such as the one described below, something I'll refer to as Avatar Visualization. However, any good relaxation and visualization technique will work, such as those by Brian L. Weiss, M.D., whose CDs are readily available through Amazon.com or any other major outlets. One of his CDs, Regression Through The Mirrors of Time, can set the basic framework for you to work with. In a nutshell, the relaxation and visualization techniques are simply a way to quell your runaway thoughts so your thinking is clear. The more playful a technique is, the more likely it will end-run any destructive thinking. Have some fun if you decide to try one. And even if you don't think there is an underlying roadblock, you can try a visualization exercise for help with a business problem.

Present Thinking for Business

You can mechanically bring yourself into the present moment by changing your pattern of physical behavior, or by directing your thoughts in a particular way. As you bring your awareness into the present moment, you'll be surprised to find how little time you spend there. And how much of your life is spent with past thoughts and future fears and hopes. When you're chasing thoughts or feelings, you're not effective in moving your business or career forward.

BREAKTHROUGH INSIGHT: Keeping your focus in the present moment, even for a few minutes, can be a challenge. It, however, is well worth learning how to do. Identifying how you feel, see and think when you are present will help you benchmark when you've drifted out.

What's interesting is that others can often readily spot when we're lost in thought, not in the present moment, something we rarely notice until it's pointed out to us. What's even more interesting is that when we're told we seem preoccupied, distant, or disinterested, we immediately come into the present, at least for a moment, because, for example, we're embarrassed. But then we drift out again, often hiding our lack of attention by asking questions so it appears we're fully engaged.

QUICK AWARENESS DEVELOPMENT EXERCISE.

Do you have any thoughts about how easily you get distracted or how hard it is to pay attention in various business situations? If so, take a moment, close this book and write them down in your Development Diary.

QUICK ANALYSIS

Did you say that you are always aware of the times when you get lost in thought? Do you become preoccupied with other issues during a business meeting? And do you feel that when it happens and you're not aware of it, it doesn't interfere with your information gathering or analysis process? If that is true, congratulate yourself! On the other hand, you may be totally unaware of the non-productive thought interferences or preoccupations clouding your thinking process. If so, you now have a new awareness to increase your effectiveness in business. Non-productive thoughts, thought static, surface when we have trouble coping with a difficult situation or when we are uncomfortable seeing what is in front of us. The blocking process can be conscious or unconscious. For example, the child of a psychotic mother is in a world of confusion. The child, for example, might be praised one day and punished the next for the same type of behavior. To emotionally survive the parent's inconsistent and irrational behavior, the child, often unconsciously, looks for ways to prevent it from recurring. Ultimately, the child blocks or alters what's happening by emotionally shutting down to cope with what is, for him, a terrifying and immobilizing world. Eventually, as the block or alteration becomes automatic and unconscious, a part of the child's conscious awareness shuts down and he loses full access to his ability to process reality. To a greater or lesser extent, our fears and our ability to cope with them create the same reality-altering process.

In a nutshell, the present thinking process eliminates past and future thoughts, anxieties, and concerns so you're fully aware of the situation you're facing. Focusing on present reality may not always be comfortable, but it permits you to keep your thinking process clear during critical challenges.

Becoming Present

Pulling yourself into the present moment can be challenging, particularly when your mind is awash with thought static. But it's possible by, in effect, tricking the destructive part of you that wants to keep you in status quo by mechanically distracting yourself from illusions and non-productive thoughts impeding your progress. Doing so will, for example, enable you to read between the lines when someone is talking to you if your gut is telling you something might be amiss.

Any mental or physical action which requires you to focus on what is happening in front of you—uninfluenced by other anxieties or concerns, past or future—can mechanically bring you into the present moment. Here are three techniques you can experiment with to find what works the best for you. See what you can discover. Keep track of what you experience in your Development Diary as you try them out.

BREAKTHROUGH INSIGHT: If you find yourself resisting any of the following exercises, examine your own personal flexibility. Business requires flexibility and taking new approaches. Your resistance may be a clue to emotional roadblocks and a need to follow pre-conceived beliefs.

Physical Technique

The next time you're walking on a crowded street, alter your pace. If you normally walk fast, walk unusually slowly. Make a dramatic change. Maintain the altered pace for several blocks. Try it every day for a week. If you don't feel like changing your pace, make any other change in your automatic movements, and stick with the change for a prolonged period of time. For example, swing your arms in the opposite direction over several blocks. Blink your eyes at a different and steady rate for a few minutes. If one change does not seem to work, do something else. Experiment. Have some fun! The point is to make yourself aware of what you are doing physically at the moment. This will drive you into the present.

When you drop into the present moment, you'll start to feel a change that you may not be able to put your finger on. It may be subtle at first. If you're outside, for example, the grass might look greener—or you may become aware of other distinctive features of where you are physically. At that time, all thought static will drop away. You'll start to see the world around you differently—in fact, you'll see the world right in front of you occurring at the moment.

You can also do this in a meeting when, for example, the discussion is starting to make no sense or seems to be going nowhere. Try moving your fingers in an unusual way as you stay involved in the meeting. Again experiment and see what you come up with. By bringing yourself into the present in the meeting, you'll have renewed clarity. Trust what you see and feel then.

In the beginning, don't look for anything in particular to happen—be patient and persist. Don't let your thoughts steer what you think the outcome will be. If the experiment does not work the first time, try it again. You'll eventually see a change in your thought awareness and perceptions. Keep track of what you experience in your Development Diary as you try this exercise.

Verbal Technique

You can "verbally" bring yourself into the present moment, a technique particularly helpful during a lengthy business meeting when you can't physically move around. For example, if during a meeting you find yourself getting edgy or feeling any sort of discomfort while someone is talking, try saying to yourself slowly at least five times, "What is this person really saying?" The discomfort could be your signal that you're unconsciously blocking uncomfortable thoughts or feelings that you need to process so your progress is not blocked. Repeating the question will pull you into the present. And then stop and listen again.

Experiment with other questions that might work for you. Again, keep track of what you experience in your Development Diary as you try this exercise. Experiment. Have some fun.

Visual Technique

You can push yourself into the present moment with visual techniques. If you're involved in a conversation which seems to be going in circles, try mentally looking at this person as though you were five feet above his head. In other words, imagine that you have floated upward and are now looking down.

Experiment with other ways to presently engage your mind. Keep track of what you experience in your Development Diary.

Avatar Visualization

As we've suggested, sometimes it's impossible to "see" where you're trapping yourself. Here's a relaxation and visualization exercise you can experiment with. This technique takes you into a clear state of awareness using an avatar, an imaginary guide—something that can end-run your destructive inner self blocking your progress.

BREAKTHROUGH INSIGHT: If the thought of visualization exercises makes you uncomfortable, make a note of it in your Development Diary. To progress, if you're not where you want to be, you must move out of your comfort zone.

The following technique should be done in a quiet place away from all possible interruptions. Wear loose clothing. The technique is done in two steps—relaxation to get your conscious mind into neutral and to remove your mind static, and then visualization.

It might be useful to record these instructions with appropriate time intervals between steps to avoid having to look at the book to see what to do next.

Getting Relalxed

Sit in a comfortable chair, close your eyes, and concentrate on your breathing.

Inhale slowly through your nose as you count to five, hold for a count of five, and then slowly exhale for a count of five through your mouth. Repeat this four more times. If you don't begin to relax, repeat the process.

When finished, sit quietly and feel your body slowly sinking into the chair. Concentrate on feeling your muscles relax, section by section, starting with your neck and facial muscles, your shoulders, and then continuing slowly down the rest of your body. Breathe deeply and slowly as you're doing this—concentrate on your breathing. See if you can sense the muscles loosening until they are limp. Give yourself time. Don't rush. When you feel you're fully relaxed, count slowly back from ten to one. Each time you count a number, sense your body sinking further and further into your chair.

Now imagine a warm breeze gently blowing across your body as you are sitting in the chair. Stay with this thought for at least two minutes. (Don't worry about checking the time; the point is merely to slow down.) Don't rush. Enjoy each step and feel yourself dropping into a relaxed state.

When you're relaxed, picture yourself floating upward, across windswept plains and finally floating down to a beautiful, sunlit sandy beach. Picture yourself sitting on the beach. There are no people or aspects of civilization in sight. You are facing the ocean. The waves are slowly rolling in. Behind you is a lush tropical forest. Imagine hearing the sound of the waves breaking on the shore. Smell the sea air. Smell the soft, fragrant scent of tropical flowers. The sky above you is a warm pale blue.

If you have any worry or concern, make up a one-word name for it and place it in the middle of a pale blue bubble in your mind. Imagine the bubble slowly and quietly float out of the top of your head and upward toward the heavens. Mentally, watch it float out. Do this for each worry or concern until you have let them all go.

At this moment you have no worries or concerns. Relax, and enjoy the feeling of the ocean breeze as it gently moves over you. Relax.

The Visuallization

When you are completely relaxed, imagine that you are floating gently through the air to a faraway place. Envision another planet in another solar system, a calm and peaceful world. See yourself moving upward into the heavens. Watch the earth slowly fade in the distance. The place where you are going is safe and free of all outer daily influences.

Don't rush your trip.

When you arrive, imagine yourself gently and slowly floating down some distance from a crystal mountain. The mountain is translucent and is sitting in the middle of a vast desert area. The crystal mountain is very high and is about one quarter of a mile from where you are going to land. Slowly and gently descend to the desert. The sun is shining down on you and the air is so clear you can smell its freshness.

Sit comfortably on the sand with your legs crossed, facing the mountain. See if you can sense the power of the mountain. It is strong and contains tremendous energy. Nothing can damage it. The mountain is your powerful, true inner self.

As you are sitting there, imagine a kindly old man in a long white robe floating down from above. Watch as he slowly descends. He lands about eight feet away from you in the same sitting position as yours. Look at his appearance. His gentle face has a soft, warm expression. His eyes are a soft blue. He is clean-shaven and has long white hair flowing softly over his shoulders.

Greet him. Wait as he greets you back. Now ask him to assist you in solving whatever problem is confronting you or in answering whatever question you have on your mind.

Talk to him. Wait for his answers. Don't be impatient. Don't worry about whether he is actually moving his lips. Just listen for the thoughts that come as you sit there. Don't edit or analyze anything.

When you think you have all the answers you need, thank him for his help. Then imagine yourself being slowly transported back to the beach.

Sit on the beach and consider what was said to you. Stay on the beach until you feel you understand the information related to you. Go over it carefully in your mind.

When you have done this, imagine the sun slowly going down, and begin to be aware of your chair. Feel all the points of contact of your body with the chair. Open your eyes when you are ready. Take your time. Don't rush yourself.

Then write in your Development Diary all the thoughts that passed through your mind while you were sitting across from the old man. These are your answers. The voice of the old man is your inner voice—a true and clear voice.

Summary

To ensure that you are always processing the information in front of you in a clear manner, always free yourself of all random thoughts flying through your mind—ones that create thought static. And the best way to do this is to bring yourself into the present moment. Doing so will automatically eliminate all past and future thoughts that clutter your mind.

Chapter 13

TEAMING UP FOR TOP RESULTS

A Team Approach for Accelerated Results

An effective way to eliminate roadblocks in challenging business situations is to work through the issues with a group of people who are open to bottom-line thinking. Here's how to do this.

Assembling Your Team

In setting up your team, be selective. Many people have great difficulty working openly in group settings because of their emotional makeup. So, finding the right people may take some doing and could involve a few trial and error group runs to hone your team. Of course, as you now know, you must eliminate anyone who blocks the free flow of ideas or who intimidates others into silence, such as people who:

• Have difficulty admitting they're wrong.
• Need to control everyone and everything.
• Are negative.
• Are reluctant to freely participate.

Above all, do not let any false starts setting up your group block your team progress.

Basic Rules to Follow

There are some basics you should follow for group problem solving. If you've ever participated in brainstorming sessions, you know in the most effective sessions everyone is relaxed and does not feel self-conscious about blurting out whatever comes to mind.

The process works best if everyone can move freely in and out of what may be considered serious conversation. Sometimes absolutely silly detours are helpful for creating a situation in which the creative part of the brain is left to run free. In good sessions, there is no pressure to measure up to a particular image or to be a certain way. The freedom to be silly for a moment is a good indication of the group's effectiveness as an interactive team. There must be no criticisms of any kind. The analytical part of the brain, of course, should always be ready to jump in to put everything into a realistic frame of reference.

So, if you want to try a team approach, you'll need a group leader to facilitate the process. You can try your hand as a group leader, but it's often best to find a good group leader with no skin in the game, someone who is able to keep everyone aware of what is happening and to be objective. Very often the best facilitator is a group outsider.

How the Team Approach Might Work

Let's take a look at how the group process might work. Assume John, Joe, and Mark have decided to get together to discuss revisions to a marketing brochure for a new company product. The conversation might go something like this with John as the group leader:

John: I like our latest brochure draft, but I wonder if the front page provides enough information about the product. Any thoughts?

Joe: John, I see your point but it needs only enough information so someone will open the brochure and read further.

Mark: Joe, what makes you think that you have put enough on the front page to catch someone's interest?

Joe: I'm just sure that we have. I've done this type of brochure before.

John: Joe, we may have enough, but since it is our first try at this particular marketplace, I don't think it can hurt to add a little more.

Joe: Oh, come on, you guys! We are wasting time talking about this. Let's get the brochure on the road!

Mark: Joe, we don't want tire marks on it! (long pause) Just kidding, you seem impatient. Is there any reason?

Joe: No. I am just trying to meet our production deadline.

Mark: Meeting the production deadline won't solve what may be a critical marketing problem. What are you feeling?

Joe: I guess my concern is to avoid having my boss get all over me for running late on production.

John: Joe, if you weren't concerned about running late and getting yourself into trouble with your boss, how would you feel about rethinking the cover-page information?

Joe: Maybe you guys are right. We should rethink it. If it doesn't hit the market right, there may be no business to worry about. We might have missed a good business opportunity.

A situation like this is not unusual. Priorities get mixed up because of personal needs. Certainly Joe is right to be concerned about pleasing his boss. His career may depend on it. Yet, pleasing his boss may not be in the best overall interest of the company's business. When personal security gets in the way of company business, everyone involved loses. The problem is that emotional issues are often not fully acknowledged. The business is best served, however, by an environment that recognizes emotional needs and keeps personal anxieties to a minimum.

Summary

A very effective way to eliminate roadblocks in a challenging business situation is to work through the issues with a group of bottom-line thinking people. But pick your people carefully and manage the process so you're not led astray.

Chapter 14

BATTLEFIELD SURVIVAL

If You Can't Change the Emotional Facts, Use Them!

Someone else's emotional roadblocks may be a fact of life in a particular situation. When they are, there's no sense in complaining. Deal with them in the best possible manner. And if all else fails, use his emotional conflicts or eccentricities to achieve the results you need.

You might feel that playing on someone's emotional or psychological weak point to get what you need is outright manipulation, which may seem personally distasteful. Unfortunately, business is an arena where nothing is unfair when dealing with people who are trying to hold you back—then it's a no-holds-barred game of survival. Unless you learn to play by his rules when dealing with him you will lose. And, if it's between your survival or his, you have to come to terms with doing what's best for yourself.

Hoping that you can deal with difficult or emotionally destructive individuals by reasoning with them simply DOES NOT WORK. Hoping that the situation will change is ABSOLUTELY A WASTE OF TIME. Thinking that they will respond to you in a fair way is TOTAL FOOLISHNESS. Getting the idea? If you think that reality is troubling, you're right! But it's the way things are. So, when all else fails and you cannot end-run his interference, you must play on the psychological or emotional issues of whoever is blocking you to get what you need or be prepared to lose.

So, if you find emotional or psychological manipulation offensive when someone is blocking what you say to yourself are your needs, consider the possibility that this may be your way of rationalizing an unconscious self-limiting agenda with yourself. Farfetched? Well, maybe not. No doubt you've already engaged in some form of manipulative behavior in a way you considered acceptable. Many people do without realizing it. It's often based on give and take with our parents when we were children. You cry, your parents get upset and try to soothe you. You quickly learn how to get what you need without any real manipulative intent. To a greater or lesser extent in later life, you may cry, literally or figuratively, as a ploy to control and get what you want.

And what about this? Remember being taught as a child that lying was wrong?

Do you also remember the first time you heard your mother or father lying to someone? If you asked why they lied, they probably explained the "little white lie" theory. That it's okay to lie if you're trying to avoid hurting someone's feelings. That explanation may have been confusing, but, no doubt, over time, you, like many others, have engaged in a little white lying to avoid uncomfortable situations or having someone face an uncomfortable reality. As people grow into adulthood, the little white lie rationalization expands to other little white lies—lies that manipulate people.

It is no different in the world of business. People refine childhood behaviors to get what they need. The lawyer often gets a client by playing on the client's fears or anxieties, as crying played on the fears of the parent. The little white lie theory is expanded in business to, for example, something we call marketing. Whatever the rationale, being able to move someone across his emotional chessboard by manipulating his eccentricities to get what you need can be a powerful business strategy.

So, when you're dealing with a difficult, roadblocking personality, identify an anxiety or fear of his around what might be causing the roadblock, reinforce the anxiety or fear and then offer a solution. The more irrational his emotional needs, the more susceptible he will be to being manipulated so you benefit. And that is precisely why you must be aware of your emotional needs—so you don't fall victim to someone doing this to you. When you know your susceptibility, you're less likely to be manipulated.

The same results can be achieved with positive reinforcement. For example, someone might not want to go along with your suggestions simply because he lacks the confidence to do what needs to be done. This is a common problem that few people admit to in the business environment, especially to their superior. So, if you suspect this to be the case, you may be able get him to do what you need by saying you're confident he can achieve what you ask, even if you're not convinced he can. In effect, you've manipulated him. You gotten him to do what he initially didn't want to do.

For most people, manipulating or cheating others to save themselves is extremely difficult, even when not doing so puts themselves at a disadvantage. What would you do if the person who taught you how to play cards cheated during a high stakes game with you? Would you refuse to play because you cannot cheat or would you cheat to even out your chances? In business, the choice may not be so easy.

BREAKTHROUGH INSIGHT: If you find the thought of manipulating someone who is manipulating you offensive, this is a clue to what may be a possible self-destructive tendency that is getting in your way.

I'm not suggesting that you manipulate others indiscriminately by playing on their emotional weak points. Doing so, without discretion, invariably can come back to haunt you. But if all else fails and the choice is between constructively moving forward or not, you must be ready to do whatever is necessary to protect your well-being. If you allow yourself to be run over, you are being self-destructive.

Controlled Anger

Under the right circumstances, controlled anger, clearly a form of manipulation, is a way to get others to meet your needs. Here's an example of how effective controlled anger can be, based on an actual situation in which I was involved. Henry, an attorney, had been approached by Paul, a long-standing client and an astute businessman, to get him to handle a contract negotiation, with a cap on what Henry would charge for his services. Henry initially resisted.

The dialogue went like this:

Paul: Henry, I'd like you to work on the real estate acquisition I mentioned to you last week, but I'm concerned that your legal fees will kill my profit. Would you negotiate the deal for me for a maximum fee of $20,000?

Henry: Paul, you know I'm very interested in doing the work for you but I'm afraid that, because of the possible time involved, our firm could end up losing money on the transaction. I'll tell you what I'll do, however. If our time charge gets near $20,000, we will let you know and we then could consider a fee cap if there is a chance the transaction still looks marginally profitable for you. We are willing to subsidize your deal to some extent after we get down the road with it. What do you think?

Paul: I think you're missing a point (sounding a little agitated). I gave you over $200,000 in legal business last year and I'm disappointed that you won't take a chance with me on this deal. I rarely ask that you do this.

Henry: Paul, we appreciate your business, but we can't afford to run a business at a loss.

Paul (now appearing somewhat annoyed): Well, I never thought you'd understand the concept. Running a business at a loss is what I'm talking about! You lawyers always want someone else to take the risk. Did you ever consider that you are in business also? As a businessman you ought to learn how to take some risk, for heaven's sake!

Henry: Wait a minute, Paul, I'm not trying to be difficult. I'm just trying to be fair to our firm.

Paul (appearing very agitated): What about being fair to me? After all, you have to risk taking some lumps once in a while. If you never stick your little neck out to work with your clients, you'll end up not having any!

Henry: Okay, okay, okay…don't get so bent out of shape. We'll take the chance. You got your fee cap of $20,000.

The interesting aspect of this particular discussion was that Henry never fully understood what Paul was doing. Paul, however, knew a couple of things about Henry. First, Henry was a frustrated businessman. He wished he could put business deals together like Paul. Henry was not really a risk taker and he did not like personal conflict. This is why Henry would not call Paul's bluff, particularly since Paul looked like he was mad. Paul knew Henry did not want to risk agreeing to a fee cap or causing an argument, but he felt Henry would not take the bigger risk of losing his client by not agreeing. Paul also knew that his legal business, although marginally profitable to Henry's firm, did in fact provide a foundation cash flow that Henry needed.

Paul frequently negotiated Henry's fee in a similar manner without Henry's catching on. Henry not only didn't want an angry client on his hands, but he also never saw what was happening. This was true to a large extent because Henry had his own emotional roadblocks which tripped him up. For example, Henry felt he was not as good a lawyer as he in fact was and was afraid if he pushed Paul, he would lose a client.

Using Another's Anxiety

Taking advantage of someone's anxiety can provide positive results. As with any emotional roadblock, when someone's anxiety creates a business roadblock, you may not be able to eliminate it by pointing it out. But, you may be able to steer the person around his roadblock by recognizing and reinforcing his anxiety. For example, if someone you're working with suggests a business direction you oppose, put him in a position that creates anxiety for him and then provide a solution that gets you what you need.

Here's an excerpt from a Board of Directors meeting with the names changed to show you how this works. Peter and John were shareholders in a company called COREX Corporation. Peter, a very anxious individual, was discussing with John whether to pursue a merger with another company. The conversation went something like this:

Peter: I think we should pursue the merger with the CORX Corporation.

John: Peter, I'm not sure it's a good idea. How much do we know about their product marketplace?

Peter: Enough to know, based on our due diligence, that there could be some product market risk, but the company's earnings seem to be excellent. I'm sure the company's management knows what they are doing.

John: Are you saying that we will have to rely almost exclusively on the company's existing management?

Peter: I don't think we have a choice if we are to go forward, and I think that we should.

John: Peter, would you then take the responsibility of determining the competence of CORX's management? If you think they can hold the earnings at the level they show this year, I will go along with the proposed merger.

Peter: Well, I'm not sure I am qualified to make that determination.

John: Peter, I am not suggesting that you make the determination; I'm merely suggesting that you take the responsibility for it.

Peter: Let me think about it and I'll talk to you about it tomorrow.

John clearly knew by putting the responsibility for the decision outcome squarely on Peter, Peter would get anxious. And, as it turns out, John was correct. Peter came in the next day and suggested they pass on the merger.

Use Market Negativity to Your Advantage

It's quite common for people to feel the problems they're facing are caused by something beyond their control. How many times have you heard a company sales executive say that business is lagging due to the poor economy? That may be true, at least in part. The problem is when the economy is bad, you can bet your last dollar many people will slack off. Some even give up trying to move forward until someone tells them the economy is okay.

What about the person who decides not to go into business because he thinks market conditions are bad? Market conditions certainly can have an adverse effect on business. But all too often a hint of this serves as an excuse to not even try.

Once a negative atmosphere begins to descend in a business environment, invariably people become frozen. However, the business person who refuses to buy into the ready excuse to not try to go forward because of bad market conditions gains a competitive edge. Inevitably, when people generally think things are bad, there could be solid market opportunities to grab. But moving a company forward in a bad market takes strong leadership at the top.

Here's a strategy for a negative market. First, don't allow an outside opinion to influence your business thinking. Use what may be an apparent obstacle as a lighthouse to avoid getting into troubled waters. Knowing what may not be possible in an existing market can be helpful. For example, if the interest rates are high, you might avoid investing in a residential construction business because the short term potential may be limited. On the other hand, investing in a business, such as equipment leasing, may be a better choice. Leasing is not as hampered by high borrowing rates.

BREAKTHROUGH INSIGHT: An opportunity can be found regardless of conditions if you don't succumb to the opinions of others.

Summary

In business, you must be able to use what's necessary when others may be holding you back—and this means manipulating them when they are blocking you, consciously or unconsciously. Believing that doing so is wrong when they are hurting your progress is simply self destructive—and something that is likely based in an unfounded belief or illusion about what you think is fair to others and to yourself.

Chapter 15

DEVELOPING YOUR SUCCESS ROADMAP

An Ultimate Process for Pulling it All Together

Now I'm going to show you how apply what you've learned using an awareness breakthrough process.   So far I've discussed many awareness insights you can use to ensure that you, unintentionally, and the people around you, intentionally or unintentionally, do not undermine your progress in business. This process is simple—but be aware that the emotional effort, at least at first, might be a challenge. The more you persevere, however, the easier it will become.   Eventually, it will become second nature and, in effect, you'll develop a healthy emotional awareness and, with that, a strategic business reflex.

Basically, you'll be gathering all the facts and potential roadblock clues as you see them, as well as all other impressions, thoughts and feelings, and using them to develop what I'm going to call an emotional roadmap. Once you have your emotional roadmap, the strategy for moving forward will fall into place.

In developing your emotional roadmap you may discover, for example, that you have a mental block when anyone asks you a difficult question, or only when your boss asks the question. Or it may occur when your boss asks any question, even if not a difficult one. And you may be able to refine your emotional reactions even more. For instance, it may happen only when a boss of the opposite sex asks a question. In any event, your job will then be to find a pragmatic way to overcome all roadblocking issues.

Throughout your emotional roadmap process, keep track in writing of all of your feelings and thoughts, particularly if you continue to struggle with one or more roadblocks, something I'll show you how to do below. In the beginning, pay sharp attention to carefully tracking thoughts and feelings, whether or not they seem relevant.

BREAKTHROUGH INSIGHT: At times our controlling personal conflicts are so deeply entrenched that we're unable to free our blocks. If you continuously stumble over a serious issue, seek professional guidance. Not doing so, for reasons other than legitimate financial concerns, is a clue to how powerful a hold your self-defeating issues may have over you.

Keep in mind: Eventually you will not need to go mechanically through the roadmap process as your awareness level and your ability to cope with changes in perception increases. As that happens, you'll find that you'll be able to end-run or eliminate progress blocks quickly and naturally as you spot them. The process I am going to show you is simply a way to realign your thinking for business so you can succinctly break down and analyze the various components you need to put into focus in order to clear your thinking.

One final point: If you find yourself struggling or drawing a blank at any point in this process, try a visualization or relaxation exercise or a present-thinking technique, like the ones in Chapter 12, to relax and clear any thought static. Unless you are relaxed, clear of thought static and in a positive frame of mind you cannot move yourself forward. Pay particular attention to any negative thoughts or moments when you're drawing a blank. Either could be a clue to the possibility that your inner monster is blocking you from moving forward.

Here's how to develop your emotional roadmap:

STEP 1: *Buy A Spiral Notebook*

The first thing to do is buy a spiral notebook. You'll be using it for the business challenge you're facing and will be making note in it of everything you do in Step 2 through Step 6 below. You'll be carrying this notebook around with you at times once you complete Step 2.

STEP 2: *Identify All Possible Roadblocking Issues and More*

To handle any business situation where you're not making solid progress, identify and write down in your notebook each issue as you see it that could be getting in the way—whether or not you think it's an emotional or factual issue—and, in the case of each issue, whether or not you think the basis of the issue is you or someone or something else. It might be something such as when you ask your co-worker for help, he always tells you he's too busy. Or the advice he gives you is usually negative or worthless.

If you can't put your finger on exactly what you think is, or could be, an emotional issue, look for clues, both in yourself and in others. And then look for ways to confirm what may be behind any clues. For example, when you ask your co-worker for advice, he never looks you directly in the eye. Or he always seems a bit nervous. Either is a clue to something that could be an emotional or other roadblock agenda. Once you have one or more clues, dig deeper—think, in the case of this co-worker example, about things he may have said or done in the past that you may have discounted. A statement like "I am not happy about my job" could indicate, because of his general unhappiness, that he is jealous of your progress or is competitive and is simply not going to help you. It may be conscious or unconscious. In either case, it could be a reason he's blocking your progress. And, in any event, you need a strategy to eliminate or end-run any possibility.

A word of caution: Even if you think you know what the emotional issue or agenda is behind a clue you spot in someone, be careful. Any unconscious, self-limiting agenda you may have could distort what you think or see in a way that makes aspects appear otherwise. For example, if someone is rude to you, don't immediately assume they don't like or are dissatisfied with you. Verify, as best you can, what you think before you act. The person may simply have other issues going on in his life that have nothing to do with you that are putting him under stress.

As you jot each issue down in your notebook, make an immediate note alongside each issue, no matter how trivial or irrelevant they seem, of:

- All immediate thoughts you're experiencing, whether they're positive or negative. Be particularly alert for negative or fearful thoughts, such as: "I can't..." "It's impossible..." "I'm stressed out about..." or "I will never get a break". And don't overlook apparent irrelevant thoughts, such as "I forgot to check the mail this morning", or "I have to get into work early tomorrow". Those can be the way you distract yourself when feelings or thoughts are taking you out of your comfort zone. In that case, use what might be a distracting thought as a clue to something you're not dealing with directly.
- Whether you think your thoughts are based in fact or on illusions (any beliefs not grounded in hard fact). If you're not sure, indicate so. This will ensure you don't delude yourself.
- Your mental state—your feelings. Don't overlook any, such as feeling happy, sad, optimistic, helpless, confused, frightened, anxious, tense, discouraged or depressed.
- Your physical state, such as being tired or experiencing tension in your neck or face.

This step is critical in the process, so take all the time necessary to assure yourself that you have clearly identified the problem and picked up as much of what could be causing the problem as possible, as well as your thoughts, feelings and physical state. And, above all, make note of everything you come up with in your notebook. As I've said, the key to progress is seeing how you work—when, for example, you make decisions based on illusions—so you consciously process all facts, thoughts and feelings head on. And, in the case of illusions and unfounded assumptions, so you don't let them steer you into a business ditch.

BREAKTHROUGH INSIGHT: What you will experience in Step 3 is something that always occurs within you when you have a challenge. What may surprise you is to see that you've lived with all of this mental, emotional and physical drama so long that you don't consciously realize it. It's like living next to the railroad tracks; eventually you don't hear the train go by.

Finally, don't worry about what the meaning behind any thought or feeling might be if you find yourself struggling to figure it out. Simply becoming aware of all your thoughts and feelings will be enough to see how you work emotionally. And that will form the foundation for the clarity you'll need to move forward.

Your notebook section might start to look like this:

Progress Roadblocks	Fact/Illusion	Immediate Thoughts and Feelings	Fact/Illusion
My project budget has been cut by 50%	Fact	Not enough money to do the right job	Unsure-guess
		First chance for big promotion down drain	Illusion
		- My boss hates me	Illusion
		- I am worried	Fact
		- Feel exhausted	Fact
		- Can't concentrate	Fact
Clues In You or Others to Possible Progress Roadblocks			
When I ask my boss for help I can't concentrate on what he's telling me	Fact	- Feel inadequate and hands sweaty	Fact
		- Feel tense when talking to boss	Fact

When I ask Joe my co-worker for advice, it's invariably couched in negativity	Fact	- Can't understand why he won't help	Fact
Joe does not look me in eye when talking	Fact	- He looks fidgety/nervous	Fact
My boss always seems to know what I have been talking to Joe about	Illusion	- Joe and the boss are talking about me	Unsure-guess
		- Joe is trying to outdo me	Unsure-guess
		- My boss must be asking Joe about me	Illusion
		- I am nervous	Fact

STEP 3: *Continuing Thoughts, Feelings, Roadblocks and Clues*

Once you've completed Step 2, carry your notebook around with you for five business days—your discovery period. It's best if there is a break in time before you start doing this—say, a day or so. The break can give your creative unconscious, your inner genius, a chance to freely mull over everything you've thought and felt. But, if you are not inclined to take a break, don't concern yourself; just move ahead with the process.

The night before the start of your discovery period, review all your thoughts and feelings in your notebook. See if anything now makes you uncomfortable. If so, pay particular attention to it during your discovery period.

During your discovery period, identify similar Step 2 thoughts and feelings that re-appear, as well as any new thoughts and feelings. Also note any additional and possible roadblocks and roadblock clues that you become aware of—whether they seem to be yours or those of people around you. Write them down immediately, or as soon as possible, in your notebook—leave space for any comments you may need to add in Step 4.

Again, take particular note of how you're feeling mentally and physically at the time of each thought. For example, note whether you are tired, sad, angry or stressed out. Also put down whether you think what you come up with is a fact or an illusion (beliefs you have that are not well-grounded in fact).

Don't rush the process, or jump to conclusions. Don't overlook a single thought or feeling detail—no matter how seemingly unrelated it appears. And if there are none, don't worry. Simply move to Step 4.

Your notebook entry might look something like this:

Additional Possible Progress Roadblocks	Fact/Illusion	Additional Thoughts and Feelings	Fact/Illusion
My number 2 person quit	Fact	- Afraid can't complete project without his input	Fear-Fact Basis of Fear-Illusion

Clues In You or Others to Possible Progress Roadblocks			
Noticed I always have trouble listening to anyone when looking for solutions	Fact	- Now I really feel unsettled	Fact

STEP 4: *Take a Break and Review*

Take a break for a day, longer if necessary, after completing Step 3. Do not think about what you have written. Again, let your unconscious creative inner genius work its magic. Then, one evening, when you're not rushed and can relax by yourself, revisit and think about what you've written. Circle in red all illusions that are in play—these must be put into proper perspective as part of your analysis so you can develop solution strategies when you get to your emotional roadmap in Step 6. Let your thoughts flow. Jot down anything that surfaces you think unusual or important—even seemingly irrelevant thoughts. Never forget, nothing is ever really irrelevant—and what may seem so can be a clue to something within you distracting you from thoughts and feelings that you need to address.

STEP 5: *Identify Past Situations and Patterns*

Now, in the evening, or when you have some quiet, undisturbed time, try to remember past situations in which you experienced similar issues or felt or thought the same way as in the current situation. If there were any, make a note of those as well.

If you see a pattern, or possible pattern, as you consider any past situation in the context of your current situation, it's highly likely you have an inner roadblock—one, if you have not yet identified, you must put in the forefront of your mind. Doing so will loosen its grip on you when you go to Step 6.

So, if it looks like there could be a pattern, take a moment to dig deeper and consider what may be a possible inner roadblock, something you'll put as a roadblock clue when you get to your roadmap.

Your notebook entry might look something like this:

Similar Situations	How I Thought/Felt	Possible Patterns
My last new project	- Frustrated, felt like looking for new job immediately - Went home exhausted every night - Started fights with spouse	Panic when pursing something new

STEP 6: *Establishing Your Emotional Roadmap*

Once you've completed Step 5 and have identified what you think are the issues getting in your way and you've gathered all your evidence, clues, thoughts and feelings, it's time to develop your emotional roadmap.

Developing your emotional roadmap will allow you to put into perspective everything you see, suspect, think and feel in a way that will set the stage for setting simple strategies to clear or end-run any emotional agendas blocking progress. In effect, it will slow you down and increase your focus so you can gain a perspective on progress-inhibiting thoughts and feelings. And to clearly see the extent to which you permit or create non-productive thoughts and feelings that interfere with your ability to effectively handle business endeavors in your best interest.

BREAKTHROUGH INSIGHT: As you're creating your emotional roadmap, keep in mind that any resistance you feel to constructing your roadmap, such as procrastination, is a valuable clue to the inner workings of your destructive unconscious, a self that may be actively creating thoughts and feelings to prevent you from moving forward.

Using what you have developed in Step 2 through Step 5, it's now time to start your roadmap analysis. Your roadmap will include potential solutions or strategies, using the format below. In developing solutions, make full use of what you've learned so far in earlier chapters. And if you need some guidance from someone—get it! Take your time, again. Don't rush the process. If you seem to get stuck for answers, take a break for a day or so—let your creative unconscious go to work for you on your challenge. Trust fully that it will come through for you.

Keep in mind: As you develop your emotional roadmap, eventually you'll see how your thoughts and feelings influence you, and you'll see behavior patterns that block your progress. All of this will be your stepping stones to find strategies and solutions to move forward. There is no one simple solution to any one problem—there are too many variables. But, when you're clear, solutions will fall into place. For example, you may find that when you are tired, you become particularly negative about any business possibility. If so, you may not be able to change that within yourself; but once you recognize it, you can learn to work around it. The solution, then, might be to defer making any final decisions until you are rested. The key is to work within your emotional currents. Not being able to give yourself the freedom to do so may be yet a clue to self-defeating behavior.

Here's an example of a roadmap entry if you discover a pattern in Step 5 to start your mental wheels turning to see how this might play out in the preparation of your emotional roadmap.

Pattern—Possible Inner Roadblock/Clue:

It seems that whenever I get frightened about my ability to complete a project, I immediately feel frustrated, tired and want to give up. On the surface I feel will suffer somehow by not finding a good solution—which makes me want to give up. I know I am hard pressed to believe that I am unconsciously self-destructive and that I may be staying in a comfort zone that may benefit me emotionally but not financially. I realize that manufactured stress creates blocks to my ability to creatively look for a solution.

Solutions/Actions:

Dig deep into what I am really feeling. I need to use a relaxation technique to calm myself down so I can think clearly. If I continue to struggle, I will find someone I trust to work these types of conflicts through.

KEY BREAKTHROUGH INSIGHT: Whether an emotional roadblock is yours or someone else's, accept fully that you may not be able to eliminate it and your only choice will be to end-run it. A solution is only possible in these situations when you come to terms with the reality of what is in front of you. By accepting rather than resisting reality, you signal your creative process to get into action.

Your roadmap section will look something like this:

My Emotional Roadmap

Emotional Roadblock/ Roadblock Clue	Action/Solutions
Can't concentrate when boss asks a question	Repeat question to boss-saying I want to make sure I understand so I do the best job
	Tell boss at the start of my meeting that I will be writing any questions down to ensure I will carefully review all issues
	Make a note of any questions I anticipate my boss will ask so that I develop a frame of reference to relate to before the meeting
	Spend some time with the feelings I have when my boss asks questions to see how often they occur
	Set up a one-hour meeting with a behavioral psychologist or executive coach to help resolve why I have difficulty listening
Boss knows what I say to Joe	Confront Joe about talking to boss behind my back Stop asking Joe for advice

The emotional roadmap process will give you the awareness and information you need to find ways to deal with emotions which get in your way. The more you work with the roadmap process, the more quickly it will become second nature—a mental reflex. In fact, you'll soon discover that certain emotional blocks will disappear merely because you became aware that they were there—particularly unfounded assumptions. Never worry about the blocks that you cannot seem to eliminate. Work around them. You will gain confidence as you push past one after another. Eventually, you'll internalize this process and it will be part of your mental reflex—and there will be no need to mechanically go through this process on paper.

Setting Effective Goals for Profit by Recognizing Reality

As you now know, an emotional agenda can get in the way of business progress—whether the emotional agenda is yours or someone else's. When it's yours, and it's blocking progress, you can overcome it if you're honest with yourself.

Here's the challenge: It's very difficult to face the fact that you are operating from an emotionally destructive reference point. Society has brainwashed us to believe that having emotional difficulties is something to be ashamed of or embarrassed about. So, we often refuse to face that as a possibility for fear something might be seriously wrong with us. Think a moment about how you feel when someone suggests that you're being too emotional. Do you readily agree and tell him you'll look into why? If you do, you're pretty secure. Most people become defensive and deny it.

So, to ensure that you're on the right track in increasing your emotional awareness so you can progress quickly and effectively, here's your formula:

1. Acknowledge the possibility that emotional issues of all kinds sabotage the business environment—they could be yours or those of the people you're working with, or both.
2. Learn to recognize clues to the existence of emotional roadblocks.
3. Accept any destructive emotional issues that you cannot eliminate.
4. Know that if you do not accept your own emotionally destructive issues, you will be controlled by them.
5. Accept that if you cannot change an emotional roadblock—either yours or those of others—you must and can work around it.
6. Accept that if someone's emotional issues are blocking your progress, getting angry or otherwise acting out at that person won't do any good. You must create a situation which causes him to go in your direction or frees you to sprint past him.
7. Accept that people who do not recognize their own emotional roadblocks are easily led astray—don't put yourself in that spot.
8. Identify the circumstances and work through all your thoughts and feelings when you think emotional factors may be involved in a business situation. In the early stages of your awareness development, it will help speed your progress if you put all of this in writing in your Development Diary.
9. Develop a strategy that will move you forward, something that, in each situation, will be clear once your see the roadblock issues.
10. What to Expect

As you begin increasing your emotional and reality awareness, expect that you will likely experience bouts of anxiety followed by periods of exhaustion—all seemingly out of nowhere. And not, possibly, for any particular reason or from any source you can identify. You may have moments when you feel as if you've failed in life or in business. Or that you'll lose everything. Or other negative or self-destructive thoughts or feelings. As these thoughts and feelings surface, keep them solidly in mind—track them in your Development Diary so you can revisit them later. AND REMEMBER: ALL OF THese THOUGHTS and feelings are ORIGINATED BY YOUR Destructive AND UNCONSCIOUS SELF TRYING TO DISSUADE YOU FROM MOVING PAST THE STATUS QUO—and OUT OF YOUR COMFORT ZONE.

Above all, know that you can push through any emotional discomfort and, eventually, you will get to the other side. There may be a few sleepless nights, but eventually, and sooner than you think, there will be emotional sunshine. And success. And above all, know as well that the very reason that you're experiencing any anxiety or other discomfort is that you are now, finally, moving yourself forward, even though from your vantage point it may not be apparent.

The Wrap-Up

You now have powerful new business awareness tools for understanding yourself and how you operate emotionally in the business environment, as well as for understanding others and how they operate. These tools will enable you to quickly see when you're drifting, or in fact rushing, down the wrong path—when unproductive emotional agendas, both yours and those of the people around you, are hampering or totally blocking your ability to achieve your full potential in business, as well as in life. The key to progress is to always be alert to what is happening. Your ability to identify and work with emotional roadblocks will improve as you acknowledge their presence. As you do, your progress will accelerate. Hold on to your hat. And GOOD LUCK!

www.ingramcontent.com/pod-product-compliance
Lightning Source LLC
Chambersburg PA
CBHW060050100426
42742CB00014B/2762